Special Events and Festivals: How to Plan, Organize, and Implement

Special Events and Festivals: How to Plan, Organize, and Implement

by Angie Prosser and Ashli Rutledge

Venture Publishing, Inc.
1999 Cato Avenue
State College, PA 16801
Phone (814) 234–4561
Fax (814) 234–1651

Production Manager: Richard Yocum
Manuscript Editing: Valerie Paukovits, Michele L. Barbin
Cover by Echelon Design
Cover photo by Getty Images

Library of Congress Catalogue Card Number 2002116440
ISBN 1-892132-40-0

Acknowledgments

We would like to acknowledge the many organizations whose events, ideas, and successes have inspired the creation of *Special Events and Festivals: How to Plan, Organize, and Implement*. Special gratitude is extended to the City of Greenville, South Carolina for recognizing the importance of special events and for providing the resources for the hundreds of events that take place each year while entertaining, educating, and helping to fulfill the lives of the event participants. We would also like to acknowledge Pam Davis for her time and support while editing the manuscript.

Thanks from Angie...
I would like to thank the Parks, Recreation, and Tourism Management Department of Clemson University—specifically Dr. G. Wesley Burnett, Dr. Francis McGuire, Dr. Bonnie Stevens, and Dr. JoAnn Zimmerman—for their time, guidance, and direction that made this book a possibility. Likewise, I would like to acknowledge the many individuals, including numerous special events staff and event committee members, who have helped to shape my life and career over the years with their encouragement, guidance, assistance, and friendship. Special recognition to Julie Zapoli and Jan Cox for their friendship and support during the long hours while this book was in progress. And finally, a special thanks to Judith Alexander, for giving me tons of encouragement and for being a constant source of positive energy and motivation.

Thanks from Ashli...
I would like to thank Keri Hall, Cindy Nelson, and the rest of the Freedom Weekend Aloft family, who gave me the first glimpse of the event business. Also, I'd like to give special recognition to my son Ivan, for being my strength and without knowing giving me courage. Additional acknowledgment goes to my family for their constant support, for believing in me, and for helping me to achieve my dreams. Thanks to Angie, for giving me the opportunity of a lifetime, and in the meantime, some great advice. And finally, my appreciation to those who have given me the opportunity to learn the business of planning special events.

Table of Contents

List of Appendices

List of Appendices

Chapter 1
So You Want To Plan a Special Event?

Special events and festivals have become common but important features in communities all over the world. They are some of the fastest growing types of leisure and tourism related businesses. Getz (1991) defines a special event as "an affair, effect, happening, notable occurrence. A onetime or infrequently occurring activity outside the normal program of the sponsoring or organizing body" (p. 44). Special events have the ability to satisfy the need for an opportunity for participation in public celebration, leisure activities, and social and cultural experiences outside the normal range of choices or beyond everyday experiences (Getz, 1991).

Events are recognized and often used as important attractions within the tourism industry and as an expression of a community and its culture (Hinch & Delemere, 1993; Mayfield & Crompton, 1995). Ranging from community concerts to multiday festivals, elected officials and municipal managers increasingly view events as attractions, economic stimulations, and part of the cultural process and social organization within the community (Getz & Frisby, 1988).

> Festivals have been a part of human history since there was cause to celebrate. Today, these special events may have strayed from their founding roots, whether spiritual, symbolic, cultural or environmental, but these occasions are nevertheless very worthwhile recreation opportunities, rewarding both to individuals and to the communities that host such events. (Robinson & Noel, 1991, p. 79)

Special events provide an element to the quality of life vital to the success of our communities (Delemere & Hinch, 1994). Events provide the opportunity for people from all walks of life to participate and to share experiences in a fun and healthy environment. Events create memories, offer families a place to spend leisure time together, provide opportunities to meet new friends, increase tourism, generate interest in the environment, and make people happy. Special events have the ability to satisfy the need to participate in public celebrations, leisure activities, and social and cultural experiences beyond everyday experiences. Events bring citizens together, giving them an opportunity to meet other people and create a sense of excitement for community members (Getz, 1991).

Festival planners and many local governments often perceive festivals as a vital contributor to local economic development and therefore frequently strive to lure as many visitors to the area as possible. Planning special events can promote permanent development in the area, thus creating a sense of central place. Matched with restaurants, entertainment centers, hotels, and conference centers, special events draw people to specific areas within a community. The creation of cultural and entertainment venues leads to new interest and vitality in the community, which in turn leads to an increased sense of pride and enhanced quality of life (Paumier, 1988).

Event Vision

The success to any thriving event starts with a vision. This vision is not just a desire, but the ultimate target for which all efforts are directed. The vision not only serves as a catalyst to establish a consensus among members of the governing board, but also defines the event's creative and financial future. The most important responsibility for the event planner is to transform the vision into a reality. The first part of the process is gathering comprehensive data needed during the formation and organization of the plan. There is a logical progression of gathering material needed to begin the planning process. Determine (1) the governing body responsible for the event, (2) the financial resources available, and (3) the time needed to accomplish the vision.

After the decision has been made to have an event, the governing body should follow a specific process to create the event. The key to any successful event is thorough planning. Whether the planner has numerous years of experience and is looking for new ideas or is someone assigned to plan an event for the very first time, deliberate attention should be placed on adhering to (or at the very least, noting) each planning step. Recommendations for special event planning steps follow.

Special Events Planning Steps

The key to proper planning is detailed organization. All events should go through the same planning steps whether the event is a first-time event or celebrating its 20th anniversary. Often events fail because an idea was created and the planning process was rushed or not followed completely. The more thought-out the content, process, marketing strategies, and financial goals, the better the chance of having a successful event will be. These steps are to be used as a guideline and do not necessarily work on a continuum. By the nature of the organization hosting the event or distinctive personality of the planning body, certain steps may occur before others. It is important to consider each step while not neglecting steps that may seem obvious or too cumbersome. A brief overview of the planning steps follows, which then will be illustrated in the ensuing chapters.

1. Design the event—name, location, and theme
2. Establish the organization structure
3. Develop the event—create the operations manual, policy guide, and working plan
4. Establish a budget
5. Develop marketing and media plans
6. Set strategy for sponsorships
7. Develop a risk management plan
8. Implement the operational plan
9. Execute the event
10. Wrap-up and evaluate the event

Using This Manual

This book is designed for event planners by providing information and resources to assist them when planning new events as well as established events. The event industry has become a profession. Events don't just happen—they are carefully thought-out plans requiring diligent focus and demanding work. This book serves as a resource, not the ultimate authority. The event ideas and planning methods are from years of experience in the event planning profession. No single method or explanation exists for event planners. Each planning organization faces its own unique characteristics and personalities. This manual is designed as a guide to help in the process and to identify ideas that may have not been considered or simply overlooked. It is meant to be used to plant seeds of ideas in one's already creative mind to be carried out in each individual process.

Whether one is a seasoned event planner, a new staff member in an event management company, or a board member for a nonprofit organization, this manual has been written to assist anyone with the responsibility of planning a special event or festival. Each special event will differ from community to community or even from year to year depending on the planning team. The planning steps presented in this manual are applicable to all types of events from large, multiday festivals to a small one-day community activity. There is no single planning method to follow—each community is unique in the organization, its resources, and its limitations. The methods and ideas presented in this manual intend to acquaint and inspire event planners as well as to help planners recognize the steps necessary to produce successful special events.

The chapters are presented chronologically, following the planning process of event production. With knowledge and experience, planners will learn when and how to combine steps, eliminate procedures, and manipulate the planning process to best meet the needs for individual events.

This manual provides many prototypes and planning tools, which serve as examples to be used, adapted, and rewritten. Every planner needs to adopt methods and tools that best meet his or her own personal habits and planning situations. We intend the text to be used as a resource and idea stimulus to help start the process, to identify who to get involved, and how to make great events happen.

Chapter 2
Event Design

Determine the Goal and Need for the Event

The first step—by far the most important step in the process of event planning—is to determine the goal and need for the event. Without knowing why an event is taking place, there is no way to continue the planning phase to determine what the event will be or if it will be successful. There are many reasons to host an event—this question is asked first before proceeding in the process. Examples of why to host a special event may include one or more of the following:

- To increase visibility in a community
- To promote an organization
- To recruit new volunteers
- To recognize a community center or facility
- To increase membership or participation numbers at a facility
- To facilitate bringing groups together
- To use an existing facility not being used
- To generate tourism
- To get a certain population or demographic (e.g., seniors, teenagers) involved
- To offer recreation or leisure needs to a community
- To promote new or existing facility
- To generate revenue
- To foster leadership development

The goal and need for the event should be written into a mission statement. This statement must clearly and simply describe the event's purpose. Along with the goal for the event, objectives need to be established to outline what must be accomplished to achieve the goal. By compiling a list of objectives (both long-term and immediate), event organizers can prioritize multiple goals. The objectives summarize what needs to be accomplished, how it will be executed, and what results are desired.

Define the Event

After the goal of the event has been established, the next step is to define the event. When choosing a special event, the choice must match the organization's goal. Filter out suggestions that don't support this focus. Decide on a feasible event, recognizing every organization has limited resources, including physical location and facilities, financial constraints, and available personnel. The event planner should make a list of types of events that would best help achieve the results in which the organization has set forth, such as

- Seasonal event or festival (e.g., Oktoberfest, Christmas parade)
- Community celebration (e.g., Taste of the Town, Art in the Park)
- "World's Largest…"
- Theme event (e.g., Shakespeare in the Park)
- Annual event (e.g., Armed Force Day Parade, National Pet Day)
- Recreation event (e.g., road race, outdoor adventure)

When deciding what kind of event or what to offer at an event, numerous things must be considered, including planning time, production cost, allotted space required for the type of event, weather conditions, time of year, liability risk, community support, and local or state laws governing types of activities (e.g., alcohol, raffles). What will be offered at the event? Will there be musical entertainment, hands-on activities, food, or nonprofit booths? Will alcohol be served at the event? These decisions must fit the event's goals and objectives. Activities should be selected to make the event unique and not just another event. In this same planning step, it should be determined what will be present at the event, such as

- Entertainment
- Art
- Food
- Games
- Displays
- Hands-on activities
- Sports activities
- Exhibit booths

Select Event Name

Selecting the event name can be both fun and serious. The name should give the event a unique identity that separates it from other festivals. When selecting the name, it should be catchy, memorable, and something that can be used again. It should also articulate the theme of the event and not sound like another event within the same area.

A catchy name can make marketing the event easier and become one of its bestselling points. If the event selects an unusual or eccentric name, it most certainly will be noticed. Event planners should not overlook ways to save the event money. For example, if the name remains the same, then costs for banners, signs, and certain marketing materials can be used year after year. Examples of catchy event names include Halloween Hoot, Fishin' and Wishin,' and Bark in the Park.

Determine the Theme

The event planner should not forget the importance of selecting an event theme. The theme portrays the event's overall purpose and goals and must convey a distinct, enticing image or quality that appeals to prospective festival-goers. Themes can change annually with a focus on a new concept each year. The theme should be indigenous to the event's character and attraction which can illustrate specific categories of event types, such as

- Music and entertainment
- Arts and crafts
- Holidays or seasonal
- Cultural and ethnic
- Historical or heritage
- Food
- Sports/competitive
- Community celebration
- Recreation and leisure
- Education, exhibits, and demonstrations
- Agriculture

An event theme can include color, experiences, time of year, nostalgia, and/or an unique feature to the area such as a food item (e.g., garlic, okra, oyster). An example of a good theme matching the event name and overall focus is "Two Delicious Decades" for the 20th Annual Fall for Greenville: A Taste of Our Town.

Define the Target Audience

For the purpose of effective marketing, it is critical to identify the target audience—to whom is the event appealing (e.g., tourists, sport enthusiasts, children, rural population or families). Event organizers often make mistakes by trying to offer something for everyone at their event. It may be necessary to be more specific, by defining a distinctive demographic, such as

- Family
- Couples (e.g., young, middle age, seniors)
- Singles
- Children
- Middle class
- Art patrons
- Country music listeners

An important reason to select a specific demographic is to match the intended audience to potential corporate sponsors' target audience. Most companies realize that sponsorships are a unique way to market products and services but want their message to reach current or potential customers. The target audience should be a measurable group with a distinctive demographic that compliments the goals and objectives determined for the event (e.g., upper-middle income families for an urban art festival). The event should try to focus on one or more targeted groups and be able to effectively market the event to the selected audience. Consideration should be placed on spending habits and pricing sensitivity with assurances that the costs related to the event fits the constituency, for example

- Little League championship game—ticket price affordable for families
- Formal ball or gala—admission matches exclusive population
- Holiday festivities—food and beverage costs affordable for fixed income

When it comes to planning events, it is essential for organizers to be cognizant of psychological dimensions, such as values, attitudes, beliefs, and lifestyle preferences, which can lead to particular behaviors. Caution should be used when combining specific demographics that may have incompatible beliefs and habits (e.g., teenagers and senior citizens). In addition, certain precautions should be used when promoting an event to an audience with incompatible tendencies than the host community (e.g., rock-and-roll entertainment event held in a neighborhood park).

Set Date and Time

Choosing the time and date is the next essential detail when planning an event. The date and time may be obvious (e.g., holiday events), or the timing should best meet the goals and objectives for which the event was organized. One of the biggest and most frequent problem in the event industry is timing—not allowing reasonable planning time. Often, event organizers are told or requested to produce an event without sufficient lead time to thoroughly follow the special event planning steps. Frequently, planners wait too long or do not select the event date far enough in advance to allow enough time to completely plan, organize, and implement the event to its fullest potential.

When selecting the date and time of the event, one must be aware of the following:

- Other events and activities within the area
- Events that appeal to the same demographics
- Dates known to the community for other activities (e.g., Wednesdays, church night; Fridays, high school football)

Weather conditions can be major indicators when deciding on the event date and time. Even though weather cannot be controlled, organizers can select a date with a reasonably good chance of acceptable weather if proper research for weather statistics on specific dates is used. Good sources to gather weather statistics are the National Weather Service, local chambers of commerce, local colleges and universities, or airport records. There should always be a bad weather contingency plan, including whether there will be an established rain date. In addition, it should be stipulated who will be involved in making the call to postpone the event, move the event to an alternate indoor facility, or cancel the event.

Select the Location

The location of the special event may be obvious or may have to be selected. Often the location is specific to the goal, such as within an area to develop (e.g., downtown or historic area), a specific location to promote (e.g., park with rose bushes, pioneer village), or the space available (e.g., plaza, football field, recreation facility). Focus on a site that can best meet the needs of the event—large enough to accommodate the crowd, but not too large that the event components do not allow for good pedestrian flow. When considering a location, a site inspection should be conducted. At this time, a preliminary event layout should be conceptualized to determine if individual event components will fit within the actual site area.

Certain factors should be considered when choosing the event location, such as

- Convenient and central location to target audience
- Infrastructure to handle traffic and crowd control, electrical, water, and restroom facilities
- Accessibility—traffic flow for both cars and people and also accommodations for elderly and disabled patrons
- Appropriateness of area for the event goal
- Facility fees and charges
- Sufficient support services, such as convenient and safe parking, security, and lighting
- Appearance and image of area
- Explicit regulations and requirement (e.g., sale of food and beverages, alcohol sales, parking on grass)
- Adjacent property owners and/or users

Chapter 3
Organization Structure

Management Group

If there is no existing event organization structure, a management group or planning committee will need to be formed. This formation of an event organization structure will vary from event to event; however, most events depend on volunteers to form the management and planning committees. Often events have both a governing body (board of directors) and a planning or steering committee.

The board of directors should be comprised of professional business leaders with an interest in the event or goal of the event. Select individuals whose professional expertise may be necessary when making board decisions or policies. Examples may include a banker or financial planner, attorney, municipal liaison, tourism agency staff member, downtown business owner, restaurant owner, parks and recreation staff member, and advertising executive. In addition to an individual's expertise, some attention should be placed on his or her community influence, networking abilities, alliances, and most important, their ability to commit to the desired time. The board of directors provides events with the mission, goals, objectives, policy decisions, vision, financial direction (e.g., budget approval), and in some cases, staff supervision.

Steering Committee

The steering committee serves in operational functions and does the work of the event. The steering committee structure is based on the planning areas for the specific event. The simplest method for creating an event management structure is to divide the planning areas into subgroups or program elements. For smaller events or events produced by an event management group, the subgroup may actually be assigned staff members. Event program elements and general responsibilities may include

- Administration—overall coordination and implementation
- Ancillary activities—plans and coordinates supplemental event components
- Concessions/food and beverage vendors—selects and coordinates food vendors
- Entertainment—schedules, recruits, and coordinates performing artists
- Finance—handles cash, accounting, and budget
- Marketing/publicity—coordinates promotional materials
- Operations/site—determines the logistics and physical needs
- Sponsorship/patrons—coordinates fundraising
- Visual art—schedules, recruits, and coordinates visual artists
- Volunteer—recruits, selects, assigns, and supervises volunteers

Once it has been determined what areas are needed in planning the event, and the committee's responsibilities have been identified, the committee's specific goals and objectives need to be determined and written. Appendix 3.1 (p. 11) provides an example of committee responsibilities. A more specific listing of steering committee members and responsibilities can be found in Appendix 3.2 (p. 12).

Once the steering committee structure and responsibilities are determined, recruitment for committee chairs occurs. Committee chairs must be able to provide leadership and guidance to the rest of the committee. The chair can solicit his or her own committee members, or volunteers can be appointed based on skills and interests. Steering committees need to set their own meeting dates and times to allow members to adjust their calendars to attend. The event chair should also try to attend as many committee meetings as possible.

Volunteer Program

Volunteer programs are an integral part of the total operation of a special event. A volunteer is anyone who performs a service for the event without pay. Volunteers for an event may even include the board of directors or governing body for the event. Most people volunteer for altruistic reasons, and because they want to help their community, to share a talent, or to be involved. They bring sincere dedication to the event. Two key ingredients to a good volunteer program are being organized and having a fun incentive package.

All volunteer services must be requested, accepted, and directed by the governing organization or event staff.

The volunteer program goals and objectives must support, reinforce, and reflect those of the event. Volunteers supplement paid employees to help accomplish tasks that may otherwise not be possible. The training, direction, and evaluation often require a time investment of the paid staff. At times, volunteers can help to manage other volunteers. The volunteer program should be organized from the top down. All staff members who will be working with the volunteers need to have input and generate functional areas in which to use volunteers.

After volunteer assignments have been identified, prepare job descriptions or project descriptions for each position. The descriptions should include responsibilities, necessary skills, required time, required training or orientation, and the chain of command. Examples of event job positions for volunteers are presented in Appendix 3.3 (p. 14). All written job descriptions should be combined into the event operations manual (see Chapter 4).

The event should designate a person to coordinate the volunteer program. It is also the responsibility of the volunteer coordinator to insure that the volunteers clearly understand and agree to their role in the event. The volunteer program includes clearly defined lines of communication, roles and responsibilities of volunteers and staff, and policies and procedures for volunteers. When working at the event, volunteers should be easily recognizable by wearing visible identification as an event volunteer and for specific job tasks (e.g., stage crew may have black shirts that read "Stage Crew," ticket sellers may wear orange shirts with "Volunteer" printed on the back).

Volunteer Recruitment

Volunteers should be recruited in an intentional, systematic method. Select volunteers for particular jobs and positions and assign them to jobs that reflect their skills, abilities, and needs. Volunteer recruitment is a continuous process; new people are needed for replacement of those who are no longer with the event and to bring new and fresh energy to the event. However, one should not recruit more volunteers than tasks. People will grow frustrated committing their time if they are not needed.

Targeting recruitment is often necessary to acquire the skills necessary for the job. Sources that have the greatest potential to be qualified and to be interested should be targeted. One should look for organizations that may share similar interests (e.g., arts) or concerns (e.g., civic groups) or are already developed volunteer groups. An effective approach to target recruitment is to solicit a leader in an existing group or business. Sell the benefits of supporting the event to this person who then becomes a liaison to encourage other members to become volunteers. An example of this method would be to go to a local accounting firm or bank to enlist volunteers to help the finance committee (e.g., selling tickets, counting money).

One should also look for existing community resources to serve as volunteers to help with the event. These groups may include

- Civic organizations (e.g., Jaycees, Civitans)
- Downtown association organizations
- Sponsors (e.g., banks)
- Parks and recreation departments
- Youth school clubs
- Churches
- Volunteer organizations
- Local college students (e.g., fraternities, sororities)

Events or organizations with a webpage can use it to recruit volunteers. Pertinent information such as dates, times, job responsibilities, and contact information should be listed. A volunteer form that can be printed out and mailed or faxed to the volunteer coordinator should also be included. A sample volunteer application is shown in Appendix 3.4 (p. 15).

Events that implement an efficiency rating system using local nonprofit organizations may see higher profits and lower losses for the event. Volunteers can be recruited to handle food, drink, and merchandise sales with an agreed upon percentage of sales going to the volunteering organization. This system encourages volunteers to be more responsible for the sales and more efficient because their organization receives direct benefits.

Numerous events use a volunteer charity program or equity program as a way to recruit the required number of volunteers needed for the event, as well as helping local charities. Organizers identify local nonprofit groups that have ongoing communication programs that include a monthly newsletter, a monthly meeting, or a regular gathering of its members. The selected charity groups recruit their own members to work for the event to receive monetary donations. At the conclusion of the event, once the net profit has been determined, the festival disburses dollars to the volunteer organizations based on the number of hours worked by their members. A specific dollar amount per hour rate is distributed to each organization.

Consider the reasons that would motivate someone to volunteer for the event and then put them into a volunteer package to help when recruiting. Why do people volunteer? Make sure there is opportunity for

- Job satisfaction
- Sense of personal achievement

- Receiving valuable training or new skills
- Meeting new and interesting people
- Doing something helpful and useful
- Being involved in a cause
- Leadership training

It is important to only accept applicants who are sincerely interested and qualified to volunteer for the specific tasks at the event. One should determine if the volunteer has the appropriate skills, personality, and interest to help the event. A person should be placed in a suitable job while also meeting his or her motivation to volunteer.

Volunteer Orientation, Training, and Supervision

Like paid staff, volunteers represent the organization and the event, so it is important that they receive proper orientation and training. Before a person begins contributing to the event, he or she should be acquainted with the event history, organization, philosophy, goals, and objectives. Supplemental material can be helpful, such as a list of the Board of Directors, event timelines, event budget, and organization structure. Ensure that the volunteers fully understand the duties required and that everyone is comfortable with the skills needed to effectively do their jobs. Provide training to prepare the volunteer to fulfill his or her responsibilities in accordance with the event policies and procedures. See Appendix 3.5 (p. 16) for an example of volunteer guidelines for a weekly concert series. The amount and type of training needed depend on the skills required to perform the specific tasks and the skills and experiences of the volunteer. It is advisable to have volunteers sign a release of liability form (see Appendix 3.6, p. 18).

Create a volunteer handbook to be used by volunteers as a quick reference regarding the event. Include contact names and areas of responsibilities, event hours of operation, festival rules, ticket and pass costs, lost children procedures, emergency protocol and contact phone numbers, location of services, map of the site, media relations procedures, volunteer check-in location and process, and other volunteer guidelines.

Volunteer Recognition and Retention

Event volunteers need to receive as much attention, support, and recognition as event sponsors. Volunteers need to know that their time is needed and appreciated. A well-thought-out recognition plan will serve as an incentive for volunteers to continue to help and to perform even better. Forms of recognition may vary from event to event with suggestions for certificates, plaques for outstanding service, an ad placed in local newspaper listing volunteer names, a volunteer party, commemorative gift, event T-shirt, or other merchandise. One must not forget the face-to-face day of the event recognition and thank you. A simple gesture, handshake, or a sincere "thank you" is notably one of the most valuable ways to show appreciation. Another way to recognize volunteers is to ask them for suggestions or advice on how to improve the event. Some events offer VIP packages to volunteers. Special perks, such as reserved parking, free concert admission, or a hospitality area with food and beverages can make volunteering a special privilege. The following list includes some ways to create a supportive climate for volunteers.

- Trust them
- Show confidence in their abilities
- Convey a desire for their help
- Listen to their suggestions and feelings
- Encourage them to be creative and to initiate change
- Show interest in their accomplishments
- Ensure they have proper working space, equipment and materials to do their jobs
- Express genuine interest in them as human beings
- Allow opportunity for advancement or higher level of responsibility

Volunteer Evaluation

Volunteer evaluation should focus on problems and opportunities. Problem situations should be dealt as soon as noticed. Poor performance or disregard of event policies and procedures must be dealt with as early as possible. At times, poor performance may be due to a lack of communication or misunderstanding. If termination is necessary, handle it with factual information and in a straightforward, objective manner. The volunteer supervisor should be sensitive and give minimal criticism to the volunteer.

An evaluation of the volunteer program requires feedback from both staff and volunteers. Volunteer job descriptions, orientation, and training need to be examined for their necessity, accuracy, and effectiveness. Consider any corrective plans that will facilitate the next year's event or eliminate any problems identified.

Appendix 3.1: Christmas Parade Committee Responsibilities

Parade Administration
- Review and establish new rules, guidelines, and restrictions
- Book float company
- Mail registration forms to past participants
- Receive registrations
- Coordinate float sales
- Solicit college and high school marching bands
- Recruit judges
- Coordinate band, dance, and float competitions
- Contract with food vendors and novelty concessions
- Serve as liaison with downtown merchants and organizations
- Coordinate food and drink vendors for parade and ancillary events

Sponsorship
- Create sponsorship package
- Solicit sponsorships and coordinate benefits
- Plan and organize sponsor hospitality areas for parade day

Volunteers
- Develop job descriptions for volunteers
- Schedule volunteers, including marshals and escorts
- Develop volunteer recognition or incentives
- Coordinate with all other committees for total number of volunteers and T-shirts

Marketing, Publicity, and Media Relations
- Create composite logo artwork
- Design registration form, promotional poster, and marketing pieces
- Schedule and organize news conferences, including invitations, media packets, and location
- Write and distribute news releases
- Coordinate with local paper on advertisement for new participants
- Coordinate with TV stations regarding live broadcast
- Design and distribute signs for parade and ancillary events

Finance
- Develop annual budget
- Oversee all income/disbursements for the parade
- Coordinate procedures and sales for vendors
- Responsible for cash pickups during event and night deposits

Operations and Site
- Design the layout for start, finish, and adjacent areas
- Design map for parade route
- Secure electricity for parade and ancillary events.
- Coordinate the communication for event (e.g., radios, phones)
- Coordinate police and road closures
- Apply for all permits (e.g., parade, tent, fire, health department)
- Coordinate hanging of banners
- Coordinate with ancillary events for site needs.
- Secure portable toilet for parade finish/start and ancillary events
- Secure parking for parade officials and parade spectators

Appendix 3.2: Festival Committee Responsibilities

Festival Director
- Oversee all operations pertaining to the festival
- Oversee overall conduct of the event
- Remain in constant communication with appropriate government bodies or other facility management
- Oversee committee chairs and operation plan and timeline

Ancillary Event Coordinator
- Plan, organize, and schedule activities to complement the event
- Determine site and volunteer needs for the activities and coordinates with appropriate committees
- Implement the activity

Concession Coordinator
- Solicit, select, and contract with participating vendors
- Control quality for all food, beverage, and merchandise sales
- Coordinate with marketing coordinator on event logo and theme prior to purchasing souvenir and mementos
- Apply for special permits, licenses, and utilities needed for concessions

Entertainment Coordinator
- Schedule, recruit, and coordinate performing artists
- Research and propose a stage theme with potential performers
- Coordinate with lighting, sound, and stage managers outlining entertainment needs

Finance Coordinator
- Establish monetary controls reflecting budget, prepare financial statements
- Establish secure and efficient procedure for collecting money/tickets/tokens during and after the event
- Project financial forecast and risk

Hospitality Coordinator
- Assure that sponsors and other VIPs (e.g., officials, entertainers) are comfortable during the event
- Coordinate a hospitality reception area, buying food items, designing the layout of the area, and coordinating the installation of decorations
- Prepare gifts for the VIPs

Lighting Technician
- Set the light levels and aim the instruments for the production

Marketing Coordinator
- Coordinate all marketing needs leading up to, during, and after the event
- Design, produce, and implement a detailed, thorough, and creative marketing plans
- Hire an event photographer
- Design and purchase event advertising including radio, television, and print

Media Coordinator
- Establish and maintain media contacts
- Maximize media attendance through press releases, phone calls, and personal contacts
- Respond to media inquiries during the event
- Set up and monitor official media headquarters
- Prepare media recaps, which include press clippings of articles or ads and commercial or promotional announcements from radio or television
- Arrange any on-site media needs with Operations Coordinator (e.g., preferential seating, parking media vans, behind-the-scene tours, coordinating interviews)
- Coordinate press conference and press briefings

Operations Director
- Oversee technical aspects of the festival, including but not limited to, site layout, site maps, venue design and construction, and schedule of events
- Establish procedures for other committees to order supplies, facilities, and other equipment
- Arrange for all purchases and rentals, collect bids, and make arrangements for on-site delivery and set-up (e.g., portable toilets, stage, tents)
- Complete a comprehensive medical and safety plan to be submitted to the Festival Director before the event
- Hang sponsor banners on the site
- Develop the event load-in and breakdown schedule

Production Coordinator
- Determine when the stage, sound, and lights are ready
- Act as a liaison between production, staff, and specific entertainer road manager
- Coordinate sound checks

Security Coordinator
- Arrange for first aid, lost children, and lost and found
- Coordinate with local officials regarding emergency response
- Coordinate with local authorities regarding police presence
- Coordinate with finance committee regarding money handling and procedures

Sponsorship Coordinator/Committee
- Prepare sponsorship packets and solicit sponsors
- Work with marketing committee to maximize sponsor benefits and to communicate site needs and obligations to operations committee sponsor

Sound Technician
- Determine if the needs of the production, and selection, and set-up of equipment to match performers' riders
- Mix the sound during the performance

Stage Manager

- Hire and supervise stage hands to unload and load equipment, set up equipment, and change the sets
- Adhere to schedule regarding stage set-up and comply with contract rider
- Coordinate with the stage MC
- Handle any lighting and sound technical situations and/or problems

Volunteer Coordinator

- Organize and recruit event volunteers and inform them of job responsibilities, work schedule, and all other necessary logistical procedures
- Assure that all releases are signed
- Distribute volunteer T-shirts
- Direct daily volunteer check-in
- Coordinate volunteer orientation and post-event party

Appendix 3.3: Event Job Positions for Volunteers

Administration
- Headquarters
- Local government liaison
- Equipment check-in

Ancillary activities
- Set-up/tear-down
- Judges

Concession/food and beverage vendors
- Beverage/concession sales
- Vendor liaison

Entertainment
- Performer check-in and set-up
- Performer hospitality
- Stage hands
- Stage manager(s)

Finance
- Ticket sellers
- Money counters
- Ticket/token weigh-in

Marketing/publicity
- Information booth
- Merchandise booth sales
- Hang decorative banners/signs
- On-site media liaison

Operations/site
- Marking/layout of event site
- Parking
- Trash removal and site clean-up
- Set-up/tear-down
- Product delivery (e.g., ice, beverage)

Sponsorship/patrons
- Hang sponsor banners
- Sponsor hospitality
- Sponsor liaison

Visual art
- Artist liaison
- Artist hospitality
- Booth sitters

Volunteers
- Set up and oversee volunteer and hospitality area
- Volunteer check-in
- Area supervisors

Appendix 3.4: Volunteer Application

Please mail/fax completed application to *Event Name*.

Name: ______________________________

Address: ______________________________

City: ______________ State: ______________ Zip: ______________

E-Mail: ______________ Phone: ______________ Fax: ______________

Date of birth (must be 18 to apply): ______________ Please circle: Male Female

I am available to work the following (please check shift preferences)

Thursday	___ Morning	___ Midday	___ Evening	___ Night	___ Anytime
Friday	___ Morning	___ Midday	___ Evening	___ Night	___ Anytime
Saturday	___ Morning	___ Midday	___ Evening	___ Night	___ Anytime
Sunday	___ Morning	___ Midday	___ Evening	___ Night	___ Anytime

Four-day volunteers will have first priority. Most shifts will be 4–5 hours.

Can you work before the festival? __________ Availability ______________________
Can you work after the festival? __________ Availability ______________________

I understand that *Event Name* will try to honor my time preferences and dates requested but may not be able to do so. I will notify *Event Name* as soon as possible if my individual schedule, as indicated above, changes.

Festival Volunteer Jobs (Please check areas of interest)

_____ Jobs most needed—assign to any job
_____ Volunteer check-in—distribute volunteer credentials and uniform and confirm job assignment
_____ Hospitality—food service
_____ Security—monitor activity along the perimeter of festival site/grounds
_____ Parking—assist with festival and handicapped parking
_____ Site set-up—site layout, equipment set-up
_____ Stagehands—assist backstage with set-up/tear-down as needed
_____ Ushers—direct audience to proper aisle and monitor assigned seating
_____ Entrance/Check-in—direct and greet festival-goers
_____ Signage—assist with placement and removal of site signs and banners
_____ Ticket/token sellers—sell ticket/tokens to festival-goers
_____ Beverage sales—sell beverages to festival-goers
_____ Event souvenirs—selling event merchandise and souvenirs

What specific qualities, skills, and experiences can you contribute? ______________________
____

Did you work at last year's event? (Please circle) Yes No If so, where ______________

Have you volunteered for other organizations/events? If so, list event and position. ______________
____

What is your reason for volunteering? _____ Social _____ Community Pride _____ Leadership Training
_____ Being involved in the cause _____ Personal achievement
_____ Other ______________________

Signature: ______________________ Date: ______________

Appendix 3.5: Alive After Five Volunteer Guidelines

I. On-Site Before Event

Volunteers are to arrive at the event site by 5:15 p.m. to check-in with the volunteer coordinator of your agency. If it is known that the volunteers will not show up until after 5:30 p.m. please let a member of the event staff know as soon as possible so proper arrangements can be made. Volunteers will not be required to assist in event set-up, but they may be asked to arrange and place the display of beverages, cups, and wristbands in the beverage tents. Cutting of limes to serve with some of the beer may be required as well. The event begins at 5:30 p.m. and ends at 9:15 p.m.

II. Number of Volunteers

A minimum of 15 volunteers will be obligated each week to work the beverage stations and check IDs. If there is an extra volunteer or two that is not needed, then he or she can relieve other volunteers.

Important: All persons must be 21 years of age. If a shortage of volunteers is known, please notify a member of the event staff as soon as possible so proper arrangements can be made.

III. Responsibilities

A. Sellers—These individuals check IDs and place wristbands on all guests. ***All guests must be wearing a wristband to purchase alcohol***. Sellers also collect cash or sponsor drink tickets from the guests. ***Checks or charge cards are not accepted***. Price lists will be posted in the beverage tent for your convenience.

B. Openers/Pourers—These individuals retrieve and open the beer from the truck. The beer will then be poured into plastic cups. Beer is not to be sold in bottles or cans to the public. Products in plastic containers can be sold to the general public as is.

C. Cash Registers—Alive After Five uses cash registers to monitor the beverage items sold. The cash registers are easy to adapt to, as the keys are preprogrammed to what's being sold.

IV. Consumption of Alcohol by Volunteers

Volunteers will not be permitted to drink alcoholic beverages while working. In general, the consumption of alcohol while working at a beer booth is prohibited. Volunteers do have the option to drink a beer if they are on a break outside of the beer booth. Volunteers will be given free soda and bottled water. Providing free beverages to friends or other members of your organization is prohibited.

V. Sponsor Drink Tickets

Sponsors and band members of Alive After Five will receive complimentary drink tickets as part of their benefits package. Drink tickets can be accepted in place of cash. The drink tickets are not to be calculated into the cash box. The drink ticket is good for any drink of their choice. Please make certain that the date on the drink ticket is valid and do not accept an out-of-date drink ticket. Before serving, event personnel will notify the group of that month's drink ticket color since colors will change monthly.

VI. Tips

All tip money generated in the beverage tent may be retained entirely by your organization. If your organization has its own tip jars, you are welcome to bring them.

VII. Volunteer Promotion

Volunteer groups may wear clothing or pins to identify your group. Groups will also be able to provide promotional material to identify your particular organization. ***The promotional material must be approved by the event organizer one week prior to the event.*** The hanging of banners at the event will not be allowed. Event personnel will provide ample signage indicating the volunteer group that benefits from the event.

VIII. Acknowledgment

I have read and understand these guidelines for volunteering at Alive After Five.

____
Agency Representative Date

Please sign your name above and mail or fax event management office prior to your organization's first volunteer date. Thank you.

IX. Contact Information

Agency Name:____

Volunteer Coordinator for Alive After Five: ________________________________

Phone Number of Volunteer Coordinator:________________________________

E-mail Address of Volunteer Coordinator:________________________________

Mail to: Alive After Five
Volunteer Coordinator
100 Main Street
Anytown, USA 12345
Fax to: (123) 456-7890

Appendix 3.6: Volunteer Acknowledgment and Release of Liability

Name of Program or Event: ______________________________

Type of Activity: ______________________________

From: ____________________ To: ____________________

Brief Description of Event

In consideration of *Any Event* allowing me the opportunity to participate in its volunteer services program, I attest and verify that I am 18 years of age or older, physically fit, and sufficiently trained to participate in all activities associated with the program or event noted above. My participation in activities and events organized or sponsored by *Any Event* is voluntary.

1. I am aware that there are risks to my personal safety or property in conjunction with my participation in activities and events, and I assume all risks associated with my participation in activities and events organized or sponsored by *Any Event*, including injuries or illness to person and damage or loss to property.

2. For any injury, illness, property damage, or loss of any other nature suffered or sustained by me which is in any way associated with or related to my participation in, travel to and from, or other activities associated with the above-noted program or event, I do hereby, for myself, my heirs, my administrators, and my executors, forever WAIVE, RELEASE, and DISCHARGE any and all rights and claims for any expenses, damages, or other losses that I may have or that may hereinafter accrue, against (list all participating organizations and government bodies), and/or their respective representatives, officers, directors, employees, agents, successors, assigns, and administrators. I further agree to hold them harmless as the result of any claims or damages arising from my participation in activities and events organized or sponsored by *Any Event*. I agree to abide by the rules and policies adopted from time to time by *Any Event*.

3. In the event that I am injured or become ill, I consent to the administration of first aid and other necessary medical treatment and agree to pay the cost of any such treatment. I hereby grant *Any Event* and its insurer access to records related to any medical treatment that I may require in conjunction with any injury or illness I experience.

4. I hereby grant full permission to (list all participating organizations and government bodies), as described above, to use any photographs, videotapes, motion pictures, recordings, or any other record of the activities of the above-named program or event for any legitimate purpose. All photographs, resumes, or other submissions taken by or given to *Any Event* shall be the property of *Any Event*.

I further agree not to institute any suit or cause of action at law or in equity, or in any form whatsoever, based on personal injuries, illness to persons, damage or loss to property, losses, or injuries, known or unknown, arising out of participation in activities and events organized or sponsored by *Any Event*.

I hereby state that I have read and understand the above-stated information. No promise, inducement, or agreement not expressed herein has been made to me.

____

Participant's Name Participant's Signature Date

Chapter 4
Event Development

Operations Manual

The most important principle for successful special event planning is organization. The key to organization is to foresee any and all specific details and then to arrange the details in an easy to follow and complete format. Every event planner should produce an event manual for each event. Divide the manual in operational segments. The event operations and policy manual contains everything pertinent to the event within one binder. Examples of items to include are policies, volunteer job descriptions and schedules, checklists, to-do lists, schedules of activities, event timeline, build-out schedule, sponsorship contracts, phone numbers of planning members, vendor contracts and emergency contact phone numbers, city official emergency numbers, site maps, and electrical grids. Instead of taking notes on the never-ending small slips of paper often lost in the shuffle, write notes, thoughts, ideas, and suggestions in the event manual.

Policy Guide

The governing board should adopt a policy guide for each special event. The policy and procedures guide serves as the foundation for day-to-day operational decisions and the administration of the event. This document should include every aspect of the event operation, including personnel policies; board procedures; vendor, sponsorship, media, and entertainment contracts; cash-handling procedures; public and media relations; risk management; and emergency procedure protocol. Policies are based on the event goals and objectives and serve as a guideline for the staff, steering committee, board of directors, and volunteers when making essential agreements. The policy guide regulates how the event organizing body will administer the business and affairs of the event.

As events grow and become more popular, outside groups will want to be involved. Have (in writing) a policy identifying what organizations may be invited to participate, rules and regulations pertaining to these groups (e.g., whether they can sell merchandise or walk within the event site and hand out group information), supplies and costs related to on-site location (e.g., tents, table, chairs, parking), and acceptable and unacceptable behavior at the event.

The first step in writing a policy guide is determining what issues need to be addressed. Event related policy issues may include

- Volunteer and staff dress code during the event
- Volunteers drinking alcohol while working and/or while wearing an official event uniform
- Volunteer limitations on food and beverages during the event
- Lost children procedure
- Administering first aid and injury documentation procedure
- Communication chain of command
- Media relations and official spokesperson for the event
- Persons authorized to sign contracts
- Purchasing procedures (e.g., cash handling, spending limits, check signing, financial commitments)
- Personnel diversity (e.g., staff, board of directors, steering committee, volunteers)
- Selling and serving of alcohol
- Waste disposal
- Food and beverage vendors (e.g., type of concessionaire, product, food storage, prices, signage, clean-up)
- Crowd control
- Sponsorship restrictions and approval
- Sponsorship benefits and costs

It is imperative that before one writes a policy statement local and state regulations must be considered. Once a policy statement pertaining to potential local and state laws is written, it should be submitted to municipal and state authorities for written approval. At times, it may be necessary to include the rationale behind the policy statement. Frequently, staff and board of directors change, and the new members may not fully understand the initial concept for the policy.

The adopted policy guide should be distributed to all relevant parties, discussed if necessary, and then kept up-to-date as things change and are executed throughout the event planning and implementation process. The policy guide should be evaluated on a regular basis. Events evolve, things change, and concepts grow, which creates the necessity to modify existing statements.

Create the Working Plan

Whether an event is a simple one-day community affair or a multi-day festival, it is necessary to plan and think about the implementation. Every event has an extensive number of details that must be accomplished before the event takes place. All goals and objectives cannot be accomplished at once; some depend on the appropriate time and money. An implementation plan can be developed by determining what approach will be used, when the task will begin, how long it will take, and the individual responsible for completion of task. The implementation plan becomes the planning staff's work plan. The function of the work plan is

- To manage the wide range of tasks that must be accomplished to execute the event
- To generate a timeline for the tasks
- To create a budget for the tasks
- To place priorities on the tasks

The operations plan will begin by identifying key elements in the planning process (e.g., layout of event, booking entertainment, equipment needs, volunteer needs). Visualize the entire event and all of its components to avoid costly oversights and mistakes.

Checklist

The event planners' next step is to build or review a checklist to serve as a guide for tasks to be accomplished. The checklist is a comprehensive assessment tool to be used as a prompt to remember these executable actions. The checklist should include the various components to be considered in the planning and implementation process. Each event organizer should develop a checklist based on their organization, available resources, and type of event. An example of an event checklist that outlines tasks to be considered is presented in Appendix 4.1. Appendix 4.2 (p. 23) is a special event plan of action for a neighborhood association.

Event Timeline

The event timeline becomes the planning guide, which should itemize any and all tasks associated with the creation, organization, production, and implementation of the event. This list of tasks includes what must be accomplished, who is responsible, and the targeted time for completing the assignment. All tasks that require future action should be compiled into the timeline. Every day as work has taken place, review the list, mark completed tasks, and add new tasks as necessary. Divide complex projects into smaller tasks and rank them according to importance and desired completion date.

The placement of all duties on a timeline can be time-consuming and challenging depending on the complexity of the event. However, it is time and energy well spent, especially for a larger event where details are more easily forgotten. It is helpful to group coinciding tasks concurrently in a logical, practical pattern that provides a general picture of assigned tasks. The timeline should be comprehensive, developed throughout the planning process, and used as a guide during planning meetings to monitor the progress of the planning committee or group.

Timelines vary from planner to planner. The key to a successful timeline is creating one that is easy to follow and presents a clear visualization of all tasks to be executed. A properly prepared timeline aids organizers by providing a complete and comprehensive plan, which will help to eliminate oversight and last minute scrambling. Keep the timeline after the event to be used the following year as a reminder of details or to be incorporated into next year's timeline. Appendix 4.3 (p. 25) is an example of an event timeline.

To-Do List

The next step in creating the working plan is to build a to-do list using the information from the event checklist and event timeline. Appendix 4.4 (p. 26) is an example of a to-do list for a road race. By assigning particular tasks along with due dates to specific individuals, everyone has a clear understanding of their responsibilities and when it must be accomplished. This list should be used during committee meetings to help planners keep track of assigned tasks and approaching deadlines. It is usual for this list to develop throughout the planning process.

Generate a Build-Out Schedule

Creating the schedule of events is the next step in organizing the transformation from an empty site venue to a participant-friendly special event. Specify times for infrastructure set-up, vendor access times, date and times for activities to start and end, entertainment schedules (time allotment for each act), tear-down dates and times, and equipment return dates and times. An example of a build-out schedule is presented in Appendix 4.5 (p. 29).

Appendix 4.1: Special Events Checklist

Pre-Event

- Appoint/select an event coordinator/planning committee
- Determine goal and purpose
- Determine location and dates
- Reserve site
- Build budget

Apply for all applicable permits
- Event permit
- Health department
- Fireworks (city)
- Fireworks (state)
- Alcohol license
- Vendor business license
- Tent/occupancy permit

Determine event liability requirements
- Secure certificate of insurance—submit to event permit office

Determine equipment needs
- Chairs
- Tables
- Booths
- Stages
- Barricades
- Golf carts
- Tents
- Bleachers

Determine communication needs
- Portable phones
- Radios
- Sound equipment

Determine electrical power needs (amps and circuits)
- Refrigeration equipment
- Cooking equipment
- Entertainment stages
- Lighting
- Beer/soda trucks
- PA systems

Identify and order site needs
- Trash containers
- Portable toilets (arrange for delivery and cleaning)
- Develop security plan (e.g., crowd control)
- Arrange for temporary parking (e.g., safe for pedestrian traffic?)
- Assure sufficient lighting for event and parking
- Reserve parking for delivery and service trucks
- Reserve parking for dignitaries and handicapped
- Vehicles (e.g., golf carts, forklift)
- Decorations/banners/directional signs

Identify water source(s)
- Vendor potable water
- Participant drinking water

Identify special services:
- First aid stations
- Information booth(s)
- Lost children (coordinate with emergency medical personnel)
- Draw site plan (show everything!)
- Establish clean-up schedule/ plan for disposal of wastewater and grease
- Establish system for recycling
- Identify streets, if any, that need to be closed
- Determine impact on traffic/businesses/neighborhoods
- Notify businesses, residents of event (e.g., road closures, times)
- Book entertainment (e.g., negotiate, approve, sign contracts)
- Contract for sound, lighting and stage
- Develop system for collecting money and/or tickets
- Fundraise/solicit donations/sponsors
- Determine what food/beverage and/or merchandise items are appropriate and/or allowed
- Arrange for vendors
- Manage all arrangements for vendors before, during, and after event

Identify volunteers' needs
- Determine volunteers' job descriptions
- Assign and schedule volunteer shifts
- Create identification for volunteers, (e.g., T-shirts, nametags)
- Provide orientation and training for volunteers
- Recruit volunteers
- Arrange for staffing of headquarters

Develop media plan
- Write news release
- Develop logos for marketing material (e.g., posters, T-shirts)

- List of radio, TV, newspaper, and other media outlets
- Identify PR support for day of event
- Determine feature stories
- Design brochures, posters, flyers
- Plan press conference
- Add event to website

Day of Event

- Ensure all equipment and signs are at proper location
- Check trash receptacles frequently
- Set up information/registration booth
- Display permit on site
- Post site map
- Test communication equipment to make sure it is working correctly
- Ensure that all areas are manned
- Brief security/police on all elements of event and the location of key areas (e.g., first aid, lost children, headquarters)
- Coordinate cash pick-up with security personnel
- Secure sufficient change for cash box
- Supervise delivery and set up of all equipment
- Inspect portable toilet areas frequently
- Supervise tear-down of equipment and booths
- Inspect event site to ensure it is left in better condition than when event started
- Maintain security until people are gone
- Send out thank-you notes to staff, volunteers, and sponsors
- Ensure that all trash is picked up and properly disposed, including wastewater and grease
- Arrange for thank-you party for volunteers
- Written evaluation and financial statement

Appendix 4.2: Neighborhood Association Plan of Action

Pre-Event

Let's get organized!

___Recruit planners, organizers, and volunteers to create a neighborhood event committee and divide the responsibilities of planning and implementing the event.

Sample of job responsibilities and committees

- Committee chair
- Finance
- Games/activities—timers, score keepers
- Volunteers
- Food/beverage
- Entertainment/decorations
- Site/Logistics—permits, road closures, parking, construction, set up, tear down
- Marketing—letter to neighborhood, flyer about event

___Assign goals and tasks to be completed by each committee

What is the goal for this event? (i.e., Why are we holding this event?)

___ Encourage sense of neighborhood pride
___ Celebrate a holiday
___ Get acquainted with neighbors

What kind of event do we want?

___Games
___ Music
___ Food
___ Hands-on activities
___ Parade

Select event name (Something catchy—something everyone will get excited about and want to attend)

Who is coming to our event?

___Determine target audience
___Is it a citywide event or neighborhood event?
___Determine age groups for activities
___Establish limit on number of participants

When is it all going to happen?

___Set time and date of event (e.g., consider weather conditions—heat, rain)
___Establish set-up and tear-down times
___Set time and location for volunteers to report

Where will our event be?

Look for the best spot. Things to consider: how convenient for your audience, appearance of location, traffic flow (both cars and people), available electrical power, crowd control, lighting, safety.

___Determine location/dates
___Does your event require the closure of a street or take place on public property? If yes, apply for event permit.
___Reserve site (if necessary)
___Secure event permit, tent/occupancy permit, certificate of insurance
___Draw map of physical arrangements (e.g., parking, stage, portable toilets, games, food)
___Establish backup plan for bad weather (e.g., rain, heat)

What kind of equipment do we need?

___Make a material checklist

How will we communicate?

___Portable phones, radios, sound equipment
___Have emergency numbers available at the event

Do we need electricity? (amps and circuits)

___Refrigeration equipment, cooking equipment, entertainment stages, lighting, PA systems

What will our volunteers do?

___Determine volunteers' job descriptions (i.e., pre-event, event, post-event)
___Assign and schedule volunteer shifts (i.e., pre-event, event, post-event)
___Create identification for volunteers (e.g., T-shirts, nametags)

How should we budget for this event?

___Determine expenses: entertainment (e.g., staging, sound, tickets, performers), personnel (e.g., security, set-up, clean-up, electrician, event management), communications (e.g., radios), food and beverages, marketing, equipment rental (e.g., tables, chairs, tents), insurance (e.g., event liability)
___Determine revenue: sponsorships, donations, tickets, concessions

What should we do to prepare the event site?

___Identify streets, if any, that need to be closed
___Determine impact on traffic/businesses/neighborhoods
___Notify businesses, residents of event (e.g., road closures, times)
___Develop security plan (e.g., crowd control, traffic control)
___Develop safety plan (e.g., first aid, food, weather, traffic)
___Assure sufficient lighting for event and parking

___Identify water source(s): drinking water, emergencies, special needs
___Draw site plan (show everything)
___Establish clean-up schedule/disposal wastewater and grease
___Obtain extra trash containers
___Establish system for recycling
___Book entertainment

How will we promote our event?
___Determine the type of promotion that will best fit your event
___Establish a theme
___Write letter/notice to neighborhood with pertinent information (i.e., who, what, where, when, why, and how)
___Develop logos for posters, T-shirts, and so forth
___Determine when promotion should start
___Establish date and time to sell tickets (if necessary)

Day of Event

It's the big day!
___Ensure all equipment and signs are at proper location
___Post site map
___Ensure that all areas are manned
___Brief security/police on all elements of event (e.g., first aid, lost children's area)
___Supervise delivery and set-up of all equipment
___Check trash receptacles frequently
___Display permit on site
___Test communication equipment to make sure it is working correctly
___Remain in contact with police/security throughout the event
___Supervise tear-down of equipment/booths
___Ensure that all trash is picked up and properly disposed, including wastewater and grease
___Inspect event site to ensure it is left in better condition than when event started

Well, did everybody have fun?
___Ask participants and volunteers to complete a short questionnaire at the event
___Record participation numbers, funds raised, entertainment booked, and so forth
___Document compliments, complaints, and suggestions
___Combine information into a binder and file for next year or similar events
___Write or call event volunteers and contracted services staff to thank them for their participation

Appendix 4.3: Event Timeline

One Year Out

- Solicit event steering committee chairs and volunteers
- Create preliminary schedule for the event
- Develop budget
- Secure location
- Prepare sponsorship packets and solicit sponsors

9 Months Out

- Send out request for proposal for equipment and supplies
- Solicit children's rides
- Solicit food and beverage vendors
- Establish marketing plan
- Apply for special event permit
- Include insurance forms
- Conduct site inspection
- Book entertainment

6 Months Out

- Meet with police concerning security
- Determine volunteer needs
- Begin soliciting volunteers
- Select ride service and coordinate needs (e.g., electricity, water)

3 Months Out

- Determine site needs and contract for services (e.g., PA system, stage, fencing, tents, tables/chairs, portable toilets)
- Determine communications needs (e.g., radios, cell phones)
- Meet with officials for site inspection (e.g., city, police, fire, parks and recreation)
- Order food and drinks for volunteers and sponsors for day of event
- Coordinate media sponsor
- Place paid advertising
- Design event artwork
- Print tickets/order tokens

2 Months Out

- Seek in-kind sponsors (e.g., soft drinks, water, snacks for participants, goody bag)
- Secure EMS
- Press release announcing event
- Order T-shirts for participants and volunteers
- Print and distribute event promotional material
- Order banners and signs
- Order awards and plaques
- Apply for alcohol permits

1 Month Out

- Finalize venues (i.e., maps, directions, and site needs)
- Conduct walk through of site
- Host volunteer orientation meeting
- Gather sponsor banners
- Notify businesses and residents
- Hold press conference

1 Week Out

- Finalize security plan with police for each day of event
- Comprehensive staff/volunteer meeting to determine any changes
- Meet with volunteer coordinators
- Review all confirmations

Day Before Event

- Set up event headquarters

Day of Event

- Police blocks on roads of event site
- Set tents according to map
- Drop off site materials (e.g., trash carts, tables and chairs, traffic cones, signs)
- Place portable toilets
- Place stages
- Place fencing for sponsor banners
- Build amusements rides
- Set up volunteer check-in area
- Place banners on fencing
- Set up participant hospitality area
- Police and EMS on site
- Tear down and clean up festival site

Post-Event

- Conduct site inspection
- Send sponsor thank-you letter and recap
- Send thank-you letters to media and other participating organizations
- Host post-event volunteer appreciation party
- Return sponsor banners
- Return supplies

Appendix 4.4: To-Do List (Road Race Example)

Pre-Event	Staff	Committee	Due Date	Completion Date
I. Apply for permits				
Event/parade permit				
Health department				
Vendor business license				
Alcohol license				
Tent/occupancy permit				
II. Determine event liability requirements				
Secure certificate of insurance				
III. Determine equipment needs				
Chairs				
Tents				
Tables				
Stages				
Barricades				
Bleachers				
IV. Determine communication needs				
Portable phones				
Radios				
Sound equipment				
V. Identify site needs				
Announcers' stages				
Soda trucks				
PA system				
Identify power and source (amps and circuits)				
Order portable toilets/arrange for delivery				
Order trash containers				
Develop security plan				
Arrange for parking				
VI. Identify water source(s)				
Water at start and finish area				
Secure coolers				
Identify water stop locations				
Spray stations				

VII. Identify special services	Staff	Committee	Due Date	Completion Date
First aid station				
Draw site plan (show everything)				
Secure lead motorcycle				
Secure bicycle support				
Order refreshments (fruit, sports drink) for runners				
Identify streets (if any) that need to be closed				
Develop system for collecting money and registration				
Notify businesses/residences of event (road closures, times)				
Arrange for vendors				
Manage arrangements for vendors before, during, and after event				
VIII. Identify volunteer needs				
Determine volunteers' job descriptions				
Assign and schedule volunteer shifts				
Create identification for volunteers (T-shirts, nametags)				
Provide orientation/training for volunteers				
Recruit volunteers				
IX. Develop sponsor plan				
Co-sponsorship				
Fundraise/solicit donations				
Seek in-kind sponsors (e.g., sports drinks, water, fruit , goody bags)				
X. Develop media plan				
Write news release				
Determine feature stories				
Design brochures, posters, flyers				
Plan press conference				
Develop logos for posters, shirts, etc.				
Identify PR support for day of event				

Day of Event	Staff	Committee	Due Date	Completion Date
Ensure all equipment and signs are at proper location				
Set up information/volunteer check-in				
Set out course markers				
Post site map				
Ensure that all areas are manned				
Brief security/police on all elements of event				
Secure sufficient change for cash box				
Set up hospitality area				
Portable toilets in place				
Place trash containers on site				
Hang start/finish banners				
Set up awards area				
Post-Event				
Supervise tear-down of equipment/booths				
Send out thank-you notes to staff/volunteers				
Arrange for thank you party for volunteers				

Notes

Appendix 4.5: Build-Out Schedule (Taste of the Town Example)

Festival Hours

Friday	5:00 p.m.–11:00 p.m.
Saturday	10:00 p.m.–11:00 p.m.
Sunday	12:00 p.m.– 7:00 p.m.

Thursday

7:30 a.m.	Turn timers off on all electricity on Main Street
	Flag railing on street where electricity works (use pink ribbon)
	Rope off flowerbeds
	Program traffic message boards for Church Street with festival info
	Turn off all automatic water sprinklers in flowerbeds and at Piazza Bergamo
	Deliver two golf carts to City Hall
	Deliver six 40-pound bags speedy dry to headquarters to put under each vendor
	Load trucks with tents, sandbags, and bleachers
	Drop barricades for main stage—Washington and Spring, Main and Washington
	Load out ticket boxes and cash drawers and deliver to headquarters
	Load out ticket troughs from Gullick Building (SE has key), deliver to ticket locations
10:00 p.m.	Block E. Washington for Main Stage
10:00 p.m.	Main Stage installation—E. Washington
10:00 a.m.	Bud World Enter Washington and Richardson

Friday

4:00 a.m.	Set overhead banners with bucket truck SE to provide banner map
5:00 a.m.	Block roads (see barricade map)
	Cones drive to Wachovia drive thru (Main and McBee)
	Entrance to Brown St. for armored car
	Put Signs on W. McBee for Festival and Bank Traffic Only
	Deliver Fire Extinguishers to headquarters
5:00 a.m.	Set tents for Friday—SE to provide tent map
	100-foot water hose and special event hydrant tap on W. Washington
7:00 a.m.	Amusement rides set-up, W. Washington
7:00 a.m.	Portable toilets delivered
by 12 p.m.	Set 4 water taps—North and Main (by Atlanta Bread Co.), Washington - Main, Main and Mc Bee and in front of Carpenter Brothers—Mark water as "nonpotable"
	Deliver 2 police stands—North and Main and Washington and Main
	Load and set bleachers (Locations: 2—E. McBee, 1—W. McBee, 2—Main and Broad)
	Put up green fabric fencing around Wachovia Plazas
	Drop 15 pedestrian fencing off at headquarters
	Drop off twelve 6-foot barricades for ice carving at E. McBee
	Load truck with stanchions, safety fencing—Load 50 Hay Bales
	Load 50 safety cones to Bike race
	Deliver 300 new roll carts—Place according to rollcart map
	Deliver 25 Recycle Carts on Laurens at W. McBee
	Drop extra sand bags in truck traffic has left on site
(approx. 4:00 p.m.)	Inspect site and vendors
4:00 p.m.	Block W. North, Alley on W. North, and E. North and Main
5:00 p.m.–11:00 p.m.	Three packers in place (W. North and Laurens, W. McBee and Laurens, E. McBee and Spring)
5:00 p.m.	**Festival begins**
7:00 p.m.	**Concert begins**
9:00 p.m.	**Fireworks display on municipal garage**
11:00 p.m.	Clean-up begins
After clean-up	Block off parking on bike race course
	Sweep Bike Race Course—Main, Broad, River, Camperdown

Saturday

4:30 a.m.–8:00 a.m.	Bike race set-up
	Set stage at bike race
	Deliver portable toilets at Main and Broad
	50 hay bales for bike race
	Deliver pedestrian and fabric fencing to bike race—Fencing at Zoo and Grounds
7:00 a.m.	Move truck out of Broad Street Station
7:00 a.m.	Check barricades
8:30 a.m.	Bike race begins
9:30 a.m.–11:00 p.m.	Three packers in place (W. North and Laurens, W. McBee and Laurens, E. McBee and Spring)
2:00 p.m.	Bucket truck for photographer—In front of Daniel Building
11:00 p.m.	Clean-up begins—Festival site, bike race stage

Sunday

7:00 a.m.	Move truck out of Broad Street Fire Station
10:00 a.m.	Check barricades
8:30 a.m.	Bike racing begins
1:30 p.m.	Take down bike race
12:00 noon –7:00 p.m.	Three packers in place (W. North and Laurens, W. McBee and Laurens, E. McBee and Spring)
7:00 p.m.	Tear down tents and pick up supplies—Start at Beattie and Main
9:00 p.m. (not before)	Pick up Roll carts—Start at Beattie and Main
9:30 p.m.	Clean-up—Start at Beattie and Main
	Clean Children's Area Last—Parking Lot beside Woolworth's and Young Fashion
	Bucket truck to remove banners

Special Notes

- Peace Center has Sunday Performance—Traffic will be around Court and Richardson
- Wastewater—W. Washington
- Headquarters—Old Woolworth Building
- Parking is $6
- Handicapped parking—Leatherwood Law Firm
- Festival Handouts to be delivered to Parking
- Need tent map and banner map
- All departments provide Special Events with phone number and beeper number of personnel to call for emergency work or no-shows from Thursday night to Sunday morning
- Ice will be on E. McBee
- Refrigerated truck on E. McBee
- Make sure covers on electrical boxes are closed
- Grease Traps—Soby's and Hot Dog King Parking, Mall 200 Alley, 18 E. North Street

Chapter 5
Finance

Establish a Budget

A budget, an itemized estimate of expected income and expenses, provides a financial road map to help an organization achieve its monetary goals. Constructing a budget of anticipated expenditures and revenue is the only way to determine if one will make money, break even, or lose money. To be a successful event manager, one must be able to prepare a thorough and understandable budget. Often planners do not want to be specific by committing dollar figures on paper; however, many ways exist to increase income and control expenses that make formulating an event budget somewhat of an art. After working out the first draft of the event budget, organizers have the opportunity to reconsider event plans and strategy. When preparing the budget, research every detailed cost and potential income possibilities. Once a budget is adopted, managers need to be cautious when spending additional monies on unbudgeted items that arise as a result of the excitement of the upcoming event. Appendix 5.1 (p. 35) gives an example of an event operating budget.

The budget can be divided into an operating, capital, or cash flow budget. An *operating budget* is a financial plan for one fiscal year. A *capital budget* is for equipment with a unit cost of $1,000 or more and has a useful life of at least two years. A *cash flow budget* anticipates costs that will be paid prior to the implementation of the event. An example of a cash flow budget includes deposits on facility rentals, printing and promotional materials, deposits for entertainers, and start-up change for food and beverage sales. One must not overlook a bank as a sponsor, or any financial institution that can provide the event with a line of credit to assist with cash flow management. In addition to the annual budget, it is important to maintain an event expense report to keep a current view of the established budget. By keeping the expense report up to date, unforeseen expenses can be identified and adjustments made in a timely manner.

Expenses

Operating budget expenses fall into two categories: fixed and variable. *Fixed expenses* are paid regardless of attendance and often do not change even if revenue falls short of projections. Examples of fixed costs include promotional materials, guaranteed entertainment fees, and facility rental fees. *Variable expenses* increase or decrease depending on attendance or other factors (e.g., food and beverage costs depend on attendance).

When purchasing event supplies, receive numerous bids or prices. A company price may vary in a competitive bid situation. Most line items could potentially be donated as in-kind sponsorship; however, remember to include the value of the in-kind item in the operating budget in case the item must be purchased. See Appendix 5.2 (p. 38) as an example of an expense report.

Entertainment. The event goals and the adopted budget will determine the type of entertainment (i.e., local, regional, or national). The level of entertainers will determine the required technical specifications (e.g., staging/sound requirements, required personnel). Performing artists have different needs and expectations that require careful examination of the performer's contract (i.e., rider). They may include accommodations, specific foods, security, and/or transportation. Include cost for mimes, clowns, strolling musicians, and any other type of entertainer selected.

Human Resources. This includes any manpower service that the event has to pay for to produce the event (e.g., event management, sales commissions, electrician, security, parking attendants, set-up and clean-up personnel).

Concessions. When selling food and beverage, expenses such as the product, ice, cups, and food storage facilities should be added to the budget.

Administrative expenses. These include expenses related to the administration of the event such as office supplies, copier, telephone, office space lease, postage, travel, and training.

Equipment and supplies. Most likely the largest expenditure in the event budget, this may include cost for tents, tables, chairs, portable toliets, communications, generators, artificial lighting, temporary fencing, golf carts, decorations, and miscellaneous site supplies.

License, permits, and tax. Depending on the state and city in which the event is held, various fees and charges can be imposed on an event by governing parties. This also includes music rights fees (see Chapter 9 for more information).

Marketing/promotions. A systematic approach to marketing and promoting the event will include print, television, radio, billboards, website, collateral material (e.g., brochure, poster, event program), event merchandise, image design, and banners.

Event signs. Planners must prepare enough signs and place them where necessary for direction, information, and pricing. One should also include large-scale event maps to be posted throughout the event site including an event information booth. Some signs that will be needed include restrooms, ticket prices, stage schedules, first aid, food and beverage menus, sponsors, specific areas of the event, headquarters, volunteers, and command post.

Sponsor expenses. Depending on the event sponsorship package, numerous expenses pertaining to sponsor fulfillment must be incurred. These include sponsor hospitality area (e.g., food, beverage, decorations), reserved parking, event merchandise, complimentary tickets, sponsor signs/banners, and sponsor appreciation gift (e.g., plaque, framed event poster).

General liability, weather, and alcohol liability insurance. Insurance is needed to cover any potential accidents or injuries to anyone at the event. General liability provides protection against claims involving bodily injury, property damage, or personal injury to third parties injured by acts of the insured (i.e., board members, employees, and volunteers when the claim stems from their role with the program). Weather insurance is optional for outdoor events that have a potential for revenue loss if the event is canceled. Payoff for weather insurance is calculated based on percentage of rainfall within a period of time. If an event serves alcohol, it is imperative that the event organization obtains liquor liability. In more than 40 states the "dram shop law" extends liability to the host if there is an incident due to excessive alcohol consumption (see Chapter 8). The event organization should also have workers' compensation to cover injuries to employees and volunteers, and the Board of Directors should have director's liability insurance to cover acts of mismanagement or bad decisions by the board. Insurance costs vary, so it is recommended that the organizers receive quotes from numerous sources to find the best deal for the event.

Revenue

Events can generate revenue in numerous ways depending on the size of the event, but could include the following items:

Sponsorships. Local businesses, media, or other supporting organizations contribute dollars or services to the event in exchange for having their name on promotional materials and/or other agreed upon benefits.

Donations/patrons. Individuals and organizations contribute dollars and/or gifts because they support the cause or purpose of the event.

Hospitality/hotel tax. Most states now offer financial assistance for events that bring additional revenues to the hospitality industry (e.g., hotels, motels, restaurants). The application process varies from state to state, but usually operates on a year-in-advance schedule.

City, county, or state funds. Local governments often contribute to events that create an economic impact, increase visibility for the community, or meet goals within their strategic plans.

Grants/foundations. Grants are usually made by public agencies or foundations to advance a specific cause. The type of event will determine the applicable grants. The grant process should begin at least one year in advance, with special attention placed on application deadlines.

Admission/tickets. While a majority of public events are typically free, many events charge for specific attractions or admission to special areas (e.g., concerts, amusement rides).

Concessions/food/beverage. Revenue earned from the sale of food or beverage can be the most profitable ingredient of your event. The type, number, and quality of vendors should be determined based on the event goals and objectives. When using outside vendors, the event can retain percentages of the gross sales in addition to booth space fees.

Artist application fees. Booth fees may vary depending the size and quality of the show and available space and supplies provided (e.g., tents, tables, chairs, electricity). Collect these fees well in advance and adopt a strict refund policy to prevent last-minute cancellations.

Ancillary activity fees. Often it is necessary to charge individuals or groups to participate in activities held in conjunction with the event (e.g., contest entry fees, road race registration).

Amusement rides/activity area. An event entry fee as well as a percentage of sales can lead to high revenue from these activities.

Program sales and advertisements. A program book can be a money maker and image builder for the event. Offering sponsors the opportunity to associate with the event at a reasonable cost can be a worthwhile revenue source. Income from the sale of the program book can be additional revenue as well as an additional way to promote the event.

Merchandise. Frequently festival-goers will want a souvenir to remind them of the experience or to collect commemorative mementos of places and events. Events can create their own festival store or contract out to a merchandiser for a percentage of sales.

Parking. If there is adequate space near the event site that can be effectively controlled, local charity groups should be utilized in parking operations, with a percentage going to the charity.

Product/service donations. Donated materials, supplies, and services should not be overlooked as a source of cost savings. One should keep in mind that in-kind donations should match budgeted expenditures (e.g., radios, hospitality food/beverage, printing). At times, companies who want to associate with the event may wish to donate an item or service that does not necessarily meet the needs of the event.

Fundraisers (e.g., raffles, auction). After contacting the appropriate state authorities to determine the various regulations regarding gambling events, fundraisers can an added attraction to the event as well as an additional revenue source.

Cash-Handling Procedures

A written cash-handling plan with procedures for collecting and transporting cash should be adopted by the event's governing body. There is always a risk of loss, theft, and error when individuals handle cash before, during, and after an event. During an event, there should be strict processes for cash sales, collecting cash, and depositing cash. First determine who will be permitted to handle a cash transaction as opposed to ticket or token collection. Then decide how much cash is necessary to be used as change or start-up cash for ticket sales, admissions, parking, concessions, and so forth. Also, it is essential to collect the cash on a regular basis to relocate it to a more secure location. One must always have security with the finance person picking up the cash. All cash transactions should take place with at least two people. Appendix 5.3 (p. 39) illustrates cash and ticket procedures for an event.

Vendor Ticket Weigh-In and Reconciliation

Many events require vendors to accept tickets or tokens rather than cash. The event sells the tickets, and then the participants use the tickets for food, beverages, or amusements. The vendor then turns in the tickets for a cash reimbursement or a cash percentage. A carefully thought-out and controlled ticket weigh-in procedure must be put into place. See Appendix 5.4 (p. 41) for an example of a ticket weigh and reconciliation policy.

Appendix 5.1: Event Operating Budget

Revenues	Previous Year Actual	Current Year Budget	Current Year Actual	Notes
Contributions				
Corporate sponsors				
Donations/patrons				
Grants				
City, county, and state tax programs				
Event fees				
Food vendor booth fee				
Artist application fee				
Commercial vendor booth fee				
Food vendor sales percentage				
Children's area sales percentage				
Beer/wine sales				
Other beverage sales				
Merchandise sales				
Program sales and advertisements				
Activity entry fees				
Gate admission				
Parking				
Total Revenue				

Expenses	Previous Year Actual	Current Year Budget	Current Year Actual	Notes
Administrative				
Office expenses/supplies				
Office lease/rent				
Postage				
Phone				
Dues, fees, subscriptions				
Travel and training				
Festival insurance				
Permits and licenses				
Professional fees				
Personnel				
Temporary staff				
Personnel insurance				
Workmen's comp insurance				
Capital inventory				

Expenses (continued)	Previous Year Actual	Current Year Budget	Current Year Actual	Notes
Public Safety				
Uniformed security				
Fire department				
Nonuniformed security				
Medical services				
Food and beverage sales				
Beer/wine cost				
Other beverage cost				
Ice cost				
Children's reimbursement				
Restaurant reimbursement				
Volunteer/sponsor				
Official, volunteer, and sponsor T-shirts				
Volunteer training and orientation				
Volunteer hospitality				
Sponsor/patron hospitality				
Sponsor package perks, tickets				
Appreciation post-party for volunteers, sponsors				
Entertainment expenses				
Performers contract				
Entertainers' expense				
Production/staging/lighting				
Producer				
Stage labor				
Fireworks				
ASCAP and BMI fees				
Site expenses				
Festival tickets				
Electrical contractor and materials				
Plumbing materials				
Equipment rental				
Site lease				
Power and water usage				
Security/police				

Expenses (continued)	Previous Year Actual	Current Year Budget	Current Year Actual	Notes
Site expenses (continued)				
Rental fee for tents, tables, and chairs				
Communications, radios				
Portable toilet rental and service				
Site parking				
Contract labor				
Golf cart rentals				
Sanitation services				
Event clean-up				
Ancillary event expenses				
Prizes				
Children's area expenses				
Licenses, permits, and insurance				
Municipal permits				
Alcohol permit				
Business license				
Admission tax				
Local and state fireworks permit				
General liability				
Weather insurance				
Alcohol liability insurance				
Officer and director insurance				
Marketing/promotional				
Website				
Program				
Brochures				
Banners and signs				
Poster				
Design/artwork/graphics/layout				
Advertising				
Photography and video				
Total Expenses				
Gross Profit/Loss				

Appendix 5.2: Christmas Parade Expense Report

	Revenues	Expenses
Commercial	$1,875.00	
Noncommercial	1,650.00	
Sponsor	5,000.00	
Cable Communications	1,000.00	
Street Vendor Booth Fees	1,000.00	
Hotdog vendor	300.00	
Brochures/entry forms		$232.05
Program		277.00
Awards and sports		147.00
Radios		625.00
Police		3,980.00
Set up fee		1,803.00
Trash		227.69
Traffic		0.00
Signs company		75.00
Portable toilets		1,056.00
Generators		384.60
Miscellaneous expenses (food)		50.00
Decorations ($129 + $21)		150.00
Jaycees		
1st place $100 prizes		
Comm march/walk		$100.00
Comm float		100.00
Noncomm march/walk		100.00
Noncomm float		100.00
Band		100.00
Total	$10,825.00	$9,507.34
Event Net/Loss	**$1,317.66**	

Appendix 5.3: Cash and Ticket Procedures

Role of Ticket Seller

- To sell tickets to the public
- To maintain balance of cash and tickets to be returned to the Auditor

Role of Auditor

- To administer distribution of cash and tickets within a single ticket booth
- To count and prepare cash for deposit from single ticket booths
- To maintain balance of cash and tickets in Auditor's cash drawer
- To serve as liaison to ticket sellers and finance runners

Role of Finance Runner

- To pick up cash from Auditors at ticket booths and deliver to finance headquarters (always with a security officer)
- To provide additional change and tickets to auditors if necessary

Distribution of Cash and Tickets

Start of Shift
The Auditor will distribute a specified amount of cash and tickets to each ticket seller. The Auditor will log the ticket seller name (first and last) and amounts distributed on the Auditor's distribution log.

During Shift
When a ticket seller needs more cash or tickets, the Auditor will "sell" it to the ticket seller.

Even Exchange
If more change is needed, the ticket seller and Auditor will do an even cash exchange. This is not recorded on the Auditor's distribution log. Cash is counted and agreed upon by both ticket seller and Auditor.

Cash Out
If a ticket seller is out of tickets, he/she must cash out his/her apron. To cash out, the ticket seller must count all of their tickets and cash in the presence of the Auditor. The total should always equal the amount originally distributed. The Auditor will recount the cash and tickets in the presence of the ticket seller. The dollar amounts for cash and tickets returned will be recorded on the Auditor's distribution log and added together to arrive at a total amount returned. The amount distributed and amount returned are compared to determine the amount over/short. This amount is recorded on the log sheet. Cash and tickets should be recounted until both parties agree on the amounts.

End of Shift
At the end of the shift, the Auditor will cash out each ticket seller. Once all ticket sellers have been cashed out and the new shift is in place, an officer will escort the Auditor and their supplies to finance headquarters.

Deposits to Finance Runner

The Auditor will also be responsible for preparing cash to deposit with the finance runner.

Preparing Bills
As time permits, the Auditor will straighten, count, and strap bills. The bills should be separated by denomination and straightened so that they are all turned the same direction (i.e., all heads facing the same way).

Strapping Bills
The Auditor will count out the number of bills they want to deposit and use a money strap to bundle them. The number of bills (not the amount) should be handwritten on the money strap. Turn money straps inside out, as amounts will not correspond.

Depositing Bills with Finance Runner
The finance runner will stop by the booth periodically to exchange the full deposit bag and log for an empty deposit bag. At that time, the Auditor and finance runner will both count the money and the number of each denomination

deposited will be recorded on the Auditor's deposit log (use carbons). One copy should be placed in the deposit bag and sealed and the other should be kept in the Auditor's cash drawer. Cash should be recounted until both parties agree on the amounts in the deposit bag.

Ticket Values

Denomination	Ticket Value
Each Individual Ticket	$0.50
One Sheet of Tickets	5.00
One Bundle of Tickets (50 sheets)	250.00

Ticket Seller Start Amounts—Sheet Sales (three people per booth)

Currency	*Value ($)*	*Denomination*
Tickets	$500	100 sheets (2 bundles)
Cash	$50	Tens
Cash	$50	Fives

Appendix 5.4: Ticket Weigh-In and Reconciliation Policy

Vendor tickets will be weighed at Finance Headquarters located at the 1st floor conference room in City Hall during the following time only: ***Day, Month Date, 11:00 a.m.–11:30 p.m.***

Tickets are to be dry and unbundled. Wet or otherwise vendor tickets altered will be hand counted at the convenience of the Finance Director. *Event Name* will use two scales to weigh tickets. The Finance Committee personnel will supervise each count. After the tickets have been weighed, they will be placed into a bag and sealed. A tag that has been signed by a representative of both *Event Name* and the Vendor will be placed over the seal. A bag will not be unsealed unless BOTH parties are present. A receipt will be issued to the vendor stating the number of tickets that were sold, as well as the initial amount due to the Vendor. This amount may change due to unpaid moneys owed to the festival. BOTH PARTIES HAVE UNTIL *DATE* TO DISPUTE THE AMOUNT SHOWN ON THE RECEIPT. ***Vendor checks will be mailed by*** **Date.**

In case of a dispute by either party, both parties will meet at specific location on a mutually agreed upon date to hand count the tickets in question. No moneys will be dispersed until the dispute is settled.

Your signature on this contract signals your consent to abide by this agreement.
We appreciate your cooperation.

____

Vendor Signature Date

____

Vendor Contact Person (Please print)

Chapter 6
Marketing and Media Strategies

Marketing

Event marketing must be flexible in identifying the different target markets by using strategy, positioning, and imaging. Each special event requires an innovative marketing plan. Effective marketing plans are not accidental; they result from an organized effort. A marketing plan must accomplish the following:

- Attract the general public to the event
- Entice the media to cover the event
- Lure sponsors to support the event
- Persuade local government to provide support services
- Convince volunteers to assist
- Encourage vendors to participate in the event

Special events typically do not have extensive marketing budgets, especially when the event is in its early years. Special events are generally newsworthy and will usually create media attention. However, event planners of even the most famous events cannot assume that the crowds will continue to be attracted to the event year after year without new and innovative marketing concepts. The consequence of inaction could result in not meeting the event's expected attendance and thus impact revenue projections.

The goal of the marketing plan should focus on ensuring that attendance goals set are actually reached. An additional and equally important marketing goal is to produce relationships with the event sponsors, as most sponsors contribute to the event for the publicity and image.

One of the first steps in marketing an event should be to identify which media sources can reach the event's target market. The process of identifying the event's target market started in the initial identification of the event's goals and needs (step one of the special event steps). Then, match the media source that reaches the event's identified demographic group (e.g., age, income level, education, ethnic origin). Events should not try to reach all segments of the market for all areas of the event, but rather focus on one target audience that would be the most effective. This method can be broken down into specific components within the event. An example would be to solicit a country radio station to sponsor a stage with country music performers.

In addition to identifying the target audience, one should learn about their spending power, their social behavior, and what activities they enjoy. This information is vital when determining ticket prices, performance times, food and beverage selections, and adjacent activities. It is also important to ascertain what other distractions (within and outside of the event) may serve as competition and may divert attention from the event. The better the audience is understood, the easier it will be to capture and to sustain them.

Marketing Plan

Event planners must discover the many ways to reach their target audience and to promote the event. The next step is to develop a marketing plan. When developing a marketing plan, it is critical to observe its budget. The marketing budget is an important element in the overall event budget, and many of its expenses can be underwritten by in-kind sponsorships (e.g., a local printing company may agree to donate the paper and printing of the event poster in lieu of a cash donation). A good marketing plan will apply every available tool to see that the event succeeds.

Next, determine what information will be given to the different target markets, such as

- Event name
- Event mission, goals, and objectives
- Event history
- Event date, time, and location
- Event organizing body
- Event schedule of activities
- New elements and activities
- Major corporate contributors
- Added attractions
- Event beneficiaries
- New services
- Volunteer program
- Entertainment highlights
- Event awards and recognitions
- Fees and charges
- Cost and availability of tickets
- Attendance numbers

Creating an Image/Brand

The event image or brand begins with the event mission, goal, and objectives. The image is an effective method to communicate with the public the goal of the event. The first step is to create a simple statement or phrase that encompasses the main idea or key point to be communicated. Then one should determine what distinguishes this event from other events. The event image helps the public and media to recognize and to identify the event from other community happenings.

Collateral/Marketing Items

The creativity of the event organizer is important when developing the event marketing package. Most often, these projects are implemented to supplement the other marketing efforts, but they end up having a more lasting impact on attracting attendees. Event organizers have the opportunity to use various formats to market the event. The following ideas are typical collateral/marketing items:

- Flyers
- Posters
- Press releases
- Billboards
- Website
- Inserts in bank and utility invoices
- Bus signs
- Table tents for restaurants or stores
- Direct mail pieces
- Bumper stickers
- Banners

Two additional marketing items commonly used by event planners include brochures and merchandising. Full-color brochures are impressive; however, they are often cost prohibitive. Before deciding whether or not to produce an event brochure, numerous questions should be answered:

- What does the event want the brochure to accomplish?
- Who is the target audience that will be receiving the brochure?
- How many brochures to print?
- How will the brochures be distributed?

After the decision to produce a brochure has been made, the design concept must be established. The appearance of the brochure suggests the image and quality of the event. It is not always necessary to include every detail within the brochure; rather, include general information about the event, such as a map to the event, telephone number and address, website address, pricing information, and event "nos" (e.g., no coolers, no pets). Often simple and uncluttered brochures are more effective. Events with websites can include the Internet address for reference to more specific information. Instead of including specific event details in printed promotions, refer readers to the event website for specific details. As a cost-effective marketing technique, some events produce a brochure (leaving off event dates) that can be used for multiple years. Also, many events are conducting business transactions through the website, such as ticket sales, volunteer recruitment, and sponsorship promotions.

Event planners can use the event image and/or logo to create commemorative items to be used as part of the marketing plan. Event merchandise lines have become more sophisticated and can be a creative method of marketing while offering a range of low-cost souvenirs for the event attendees, such as clothing, pins and buttons, posters, and cups. Remember that an event must secure protection for its name, image, logo, and designs in the form of copyrights and trademarks.

Media Partnerships

Establishing a strong relationship with the media is key to building an audience, creating interest, and generating support for the event. The goal of media partnerships is to increase event traffic and sales and to build the events' brand awareness. An event can be very attractive to the media, especially if the event is known on a regional or national level. Often the media will request to be a part of the event by way of trading promotional announcements for the naming rights of a special area within the event (e.g., WXYZ Radio Children's Area). Media may even trade promotional services in exchange for space at the event. Many successful events are in the position to request a written proposal from the media indicating the number and length of promotional announcements, dates, and times. Depending on the proposed promotional schedule, the media source can be matched with an appropriate sponsorship package. Chapter 7 includes a more detailed description of a media sponsorship. Typical media partnerships with events involve trading in-kind services for promotion of the event. Examples may include:

- Using a media personality as Master of Ceremonies for stages or ancillary events
- Promotional or ticket giveaways
- On-air interviews with event organizers and/or benefiting charity
- Printing the event program

Obtain written agreements with all media partners to include the event corporate sponsors within their promotions. For example, one of the benefits for the title sponsor includes that the sponsor's name is built into the event name (e.g., *Our Town Bank* Arts Festival); therefore, the media partner must agree to uphold the event name to participate in the event. Appendix 6.1 (p. 47) presents an example of a radio station sponsorship agreement.

Promotions

Event planners may wish to add value to their special event by implementing promotions, created to further enhance marketing efforts. This includes any actions used to get the word out regarding the event. Examples include paid advertising, public service announcements, on-air interviews, news articles, posters, flyers, webpages, billboards, and public networking. Additional promotions may involve contests, call-in-to-win giveaways, and celebrity endorsements. Media partnerships can be essential to the success of the promotional campaigns.

Publicity

Often, organizers rely on the free publicity of the promotions as an effective and cost-saving means of marketing the event; however, it is totally uncontrolled. Investigate the many ways that the event can be promoted at no cost to the event. One key principle in event marketing is to not pay for something when it can be free. The amount of publicity depends on how one develops this area and how well the event planner follows through. One must be aggressive and remember all that they can do is say no. Examples of free publicity include

- Public service announcements
- Radio and television talk shows
- Listing on cable or municipal television networks
- Feature stories

Public Service Announcements

Public service announcements are used to pursue positive, targeted media attention for the event. This can be accomplished by developing and presenting exciting, unique, and interesting elements pertaining to the event. Any unusual happening or human-interest angle generally attracts the media's attention. Getting the media to run information regarding the event depends on the creativity, content, and presentation of a media release. A well-written release will enlist the media's interest in covering the event.

Many months before the event, one should prepare a media list to include for each organization the contact person's name, position, address, phone number, fax number, and e-mail address. To get started, the event planner should visit the library or find websites with media directories for the area. Then, one should call and confirm that the contact information is still accurate. This will save the organizer time when sending out the release. Tips for writing a media release include the following:

- Type double-spaced on 8.5" x 11" white paper
- Include the contact person's name, phone number, and e-mail address
- Include current date and release date or "For Immediate Release"
- In all capital letters, center the headline for the release
- Begin the first paragraph with the city and state where the event is to be held
- If the release is more than one page, write "More" at the bottom of the page and number the following pages (include header/footer with event name)
- Indicate the end of the story with ### or END after the last paragraph, centered on the page

The release should be written with the most important information first and then follow with secondary details. This allows editors to "cut" the release at any time and still preserve the most important information about the event. Be concise and to the point by staying with the facts of the event and refraining from embellishing and using slang terms. Make sure all of the information is correct before it is sent. There is nothing more disturbing than sending out a release with the wrong information. At least three people should proof any media notice before it is released. Appendix 6.2 (p. 50) displays an example of a media release. A media release can be part of a media kit to draw extra attention to the event or to provide additional information to the media sources. A media kit may include the following:

- Contact names/addresses
- Organization information
- Event history
- Profiles of event benefactors
- Detailed schedules of the event
- Biographies of key entertainers
- Black and white photographs of entertainers
- New elements of the event
- Photos, video, and logos of the event

Advertising

Purchasing space or time from a media source that exposes a message to a targeted audience is advertising. Usually due to limited advertising budgets, events do not depend on paid advertisements unless conventional promotions are not available or are not reaching the target audience. A word of warning: Once an event purchases advertising from any specific media source, it will be difficult to revert back to obtaining free publicity from that media source or others in the region. Also, event organizers should carefully evaluate whether the cost of the advertising to be purchased will actually result in an increase of festival attendees or net profit. Examples of paid advertisements may include

- Radio commercials
- Television commercials

- Newspaper ads or inserts
- Magazine ads
- Billboards
- Website
- Sandwich boards
- Aerial
- Mall kiosks
- Transit

With proper knowledge and planning, event planners can make the most of their cash investment. To begin the process of purchasing advertisements, first obtain a rate card (which includes ad costs for times/channels) from the media sales representative. It is not always necessary to pay rate card prices—use negotiating skills and sponsorship offers to obtain better rates and position. In addition, an organization that produces several events per year might be able to negotiate a frequency discount from the advertiser. When purchasing advertisements, evaluate the following:

- Frequency—How often will the advertisement run?
- Time frame—What dates will the ad run? For broadcast advertisement, what parts of the day will effectively reach the target audience?
- Size of the advertisement
- Placement of the advertisement (e.g., time of day, page)
- Target audience—What are the demographics of the advertiser? Will their target audience reach your target audience?

Evaluating the Marketing Plan

It is important to develop a means to evaluate the marketing program to determine if methods and strategies were effective. Organizers should evaluate each marketing element to conclude its effectiveness and if it reached the intended audience. If the event advertised advanced ticket sales, was there an increase in sales after an advertisement ran? Did the media and marketing efforts reach the target audience? Many event planners find it useful to chart sales in relation to the timing of different ads.

Planners must keep track of all publicity the event receives to support the marketing plan evaluation. This is accomplished by recording the type of media (e.g., television, newspaper, editorials), dates, subject of the story, and copies of news articles or tapes of coverage. Also, sponsors will need this recap of publicity, which they received by way of the event marketing.

Appendix 6.1: Radio Station Sponsorship Agreement

THIS AGREEMENT, made and entered into effective as of the ________ day of ____________________, 20____, by and between a corporate organization under the laws of *Name of State* (hereinafter "Manager") and ____, a *Name of State* corporation (hereinafter "Sponsor").

WHEREAS, Manager, either individually or in cooperation with one or more other parties, will host, put on, organize, arrange for, back, sponsor, participate in, or otherwise cause to come about, or play an active role in the coming about, of the below referenced cultural and/or entertainment event in the *City of Anywhere*, such event hereinafter referred to as "Event"; and

WHEREAS, Manager and Sponsor desire to enter into a suitable arrangement whereby Sponsor will back or otherwise sponsor said Event.

NOW, THEREFORE, in consideration of the foregoing, the parties hereto agree as follows:

1.

The Event shall be as shown in this Section 1.

Event ____
Date(s) ____
Location ____
Time ____

2.

During the term of this Agreement, Sponsor shall be considered an official radio station of the Event, and to the extent that Manager has the right to do so and only to such extent, Manager hereby grants to Sponsor the right to use any official Event logo in advertising and promoting Sponsor's station in conjunction with the advertisement of said Event, as more specifically set out in the following sections; provided that Manager, in its sole discretion, shall always have the right to determine the propriety of Sponsor's use of any Event logo. Should Manager determine, in its sole discretion, that Sponsor's use of the Event logo is unsuitable, then, upon direction by Manager, Sponsor shall alter its use of the Event logo to a use considered suitable by Manager, or cease use of the Event logo altogether.

3.

Manager shall use its best efforts to afford Sponsor the opportunity to put up a total of _____ banners at the Event, each banner measuring no larger than __________________________, at locations to be mutually agreed upon by Manager and Sponsor. If Manager and Sponsor are unable to agree upon a location for said banners, then the banners shall be placed at locations of Manager's choosing.

4.

Sponsor shall run on its radio station a schedule of commercials, the content of which has been approved by Manager, to advertise the Event. The number of radio commercials which Sponsor shall run, and the schedule for same, shall be confirmed in writing to Manager at least two weeks prior to the Event, and shall be as set out in this Section 4, as follows:

Date commercials to begin ______________________________________

Date commercials to end ______________________________________

Minimum number of commercials per day, with exact times to be supplied later by Sponsor ______________________________________

Total cash value of commercials ______________________________________

Affidavit to be provided by ______________________________________

5.

It is understood and agreed by the parties hereto that one or more stages may be set up at the Event for the performance of live entertainment during the Event. Manager and Sponsor shall have the right to mutually agree whether or not Sponsor shall, individually or in conjunction with one or more other parties, sponsor the performances at an Event stage. If it is agreed that Sponsor will be a sponsor for an Event stage, then Sponsor will submit to Manager a list of performers that Sponsor thinks would be suitable for the Event stage that it will sponsor. However, the final determination of which performers will perform at an Event stage shall be the sole right and responsibility of Manager, or its designee.

Sponsor is encouraged, though not required, to have its personnel host (MC) any Event stage which it sponsors. If Sponsor does host (MC) an Event stage, then Sponsor agrees to make reasonable announcements relative to the Event that are requested by Manager. Manager agrees that it will use its best efforts not to abuse this right.

As Sponsor is in the business of dealing routinely with performers, Sponsor is requested, though not required, to use its contacts to secure the best contractual arrangements with performers for the Event, and Sponsor will work closely with Manager in doing so. However, the foregoing not withstanding, the final determination of which performers shall perform at the Event, either on an Event stage or off, and the terms of the contract(s) for such performer(s), shall be the sole right and responsibility of Manager; and no performer or artist shall appear, or be advertised to appear, at the Event without the express written consent of Manager.

All scheduling for all performances at the Event, either on an Event stage or off, shall be done by Manager or its designee, and no alterations to such schedule shall be made without the consent of Manager or its designee.

Sponsor shall not be permitted to broadcast over the radio from a location adjacent to any Event stage while a performance is ongoing at such stage without the express consent of Manager or its designee. Further, should any radio broadcast by Sponsor be shown to cause technical interference with any Event performance during sound checks, then Sponsor shall turn its broadcast volume down to a level that will not cause such interference. Should Manager determine, in its sole discretion, that such interference is not adequately relieved, then Manager shall have the right to require Sponsor to further turn down the volume of its broadcast, or to cease such remote broadcast altogether.

Manager will use its best efforts not to place Sponsor in physical proximity to any other radio station, or to an Event stage, such that Sponsor will not be allowed to use a reasonable volume for its broadcasts.

6.

Sponsor is cautioned to be mindful that the solicitation of exceptionally large groups of listeners for promotional purposes can have a taxing and detrimental effect upon the limited resources of Event security and management. Should Sponsor solicit and cause a group of listeners to gather, the numbers of which cause the Event to incur additional costs for security and/or operation, then Sponsor agrees to pay a reasonable charge for same. Additionally, Manager reserves the right at all times to require Sponsor to cease such broadcasts should Manager, in its sole discretion, determine that such is necessary.

7.

Exclusivity and Ambush Protection—The Manager reserves the right to protect all Event sponsors from cosponsorship of the Event. Any cosponsorship of the Event produced by the Radio Station and other sponsors are prohibited without the expressed written consent of the Manager. The Manager reserves the right to cosponsor any area not in conflict of the current sponsor.

8.

Satisfactory sponsorship of an Event by Sponsor hereunder shall give Sponsor the option to apply to Manager for the sponsorship of said Event in subsequent years, if any, and Manager shall grant Sponsor the right to sponsor said Event for subsequent years, if any, unless Manager determines, in its sole discretion, that such sponsorship is not in the best interests of the Event.

9.

In addition to the foregoing, Sponsor agrees to pay to Manager a cash contribution of $________ for the sponsorship of the Event, said cash contribution to be delivered to Manager within 15 days of the commencement of the Event.

10.

Sponsor shall indemnify and hold harmless Manager, its officers, directors, employees, representatives, sponsors, contractors and/or agents from and against any and all claims, suits or actions for damages to property and/or injury to persons, including death, resulting or in any way arising from the acts or omissions hereunder of Sponsor or its employees, agents, representatives, patrons, or guests.

11.

Manager's Requirements—Manager and Event agree to the following terms and conditions:

Manager to provide:

Location for remote broadcasts: Yes _____ No _____ Describe: ____

Electrical Power (One 20-amp circuit): Yes _____ No _____

Stage Sponsorship: Yes _____ No _____ Describe: ____

Tent, tables, chairs: Yes _____ No _____ Describe: ____
(e.g., 10-foot by 10-foot tent, one 8-foot table, and two chairs = $100)

Other event benefits: ____

____

____

12.

This Agreement shall extend from the effective date herein until the termination of the Event, provided that Sponsor shall not be relieved of any liability or obligation arising prior to the termination of this Agreement, including but not limited to the indemnity provisions set out herein.

13.

The rights and obligations herein shall inure to and be binding upon the successors and assigns of the parties hereto.

WITNESSES:

____

____

MANAGER, ORGANIZATION NAME

By ____
John Doe, Executive Director

WITNESSES:

____

____

SPONSOR
By: ____

Title: ____

Radio station: ____

Appendix 6.2: Media Release

Date: February 1, 20___

For Immediate Release—Run through April 30, 20___

From: Ms. Susie Que
Marketing Coordinator, Events Management, Inc., Anytown, USA
Phone: 123–555–1234, FAX: 123–555–1235

ALIVE DOWNTOWN RETURNS FOR ANOTHER SEASON

Anytown, USA—Alive Downtown, a major fundraiser for the Develop Downtown Council (DDC) returns for another season. This event provides critical revenue for DDC and projects that benefit downtown beautification projects, public sculpture, and downtown promotions.

Alive Downtown is a traditional, weekly music series that was established to attract the downtown business workers after hours to socialize and patronize the local eateries. Featuring weekly live entertainment, Alive Down town integrates and promotes the DDC and their supported projects. Joe Brown, Executive Director for Events Management, Inc. said, "Events Management, Inc. is once again honored to manage one of Anytown's most exciting events and look forward to this year's entertainment lineup."

Alive Downtown is scheduled every Thursday night, April 5 through October 4, 20___, from 5:00 p.m. to 9:00 p.m. The weekly event is held in downtown plaza, at the corner of N. Main and 17th Streets, in downtown Anytown, USA.

# # #

Chapter 7
Sponsorships

When organizing a special event, few areas are more significant and more difficult than sponsorships. Sponsorship can be defined as a monetary or in-kind contribution for the purpose of publicity, advertising, or promotion. Most events of any size, whether local, national, or international, could not survive without some contributions from commercial businesses and individuals. Often event revenues are not enough to cover the entire event cost. A commercial sponsorship program helps an event to cover costs, to lessen participant fees and charges, and to secure the longevity of the event. Sponsorship donations have become the backbone of today's events and frequently determine their quality, size, and success.

A business may choose to sponsor an event for many reasons. The most common sponsorship motivation is the marketing benefits. Sponsors are interested in opportunities to create business and to increase sales. Event sponsorship can increase business before and after an event, create product identification, develop brand loyalty, and acquire potential customers. Some companies, especially local sponsors, participate in an event for public goodwill, to demonstrate community support, and to be good corporate citizens. Also, at times, businesses contribute to an event to strengthen the company image and to impress community leaders and VIPs. Why do companies sponsor events?

- Enhanced image/public awareness/branding
- Good publicity
- Opportunity to make a contribution to community (i.e., be a good corporate citizen)
- Promotion of new product or service
- Test market
- On-site sampling of product/merchandising
- Expand use of current product/services
- Increase sales
- Improve customer relations
- Employee or customer incentive
- Corporate hospitality
- Associate with a specific lifestyle or demographic (e.g., healthy lifestyle, seniors)

Sponsorship Opportunities

The first step in obtaining sponsors is to identify the sponsorship opportunities at the event. Event planners must determine what the event is worth to the sponsor, the available opportunities for brand promotion and/or sales, and whether there will be media exposure attached to the sponsorship. This can be achieved by making an inventory of all sellable event components, such as

- Ticket booths
- Stages
- Children's area
- Food court
- Naming of event components
- Hospitality area
- Back of tickets
- Naming rights on promotional material: maps, flyers, brochures, posters, billboards

The next step in building a sponsorship program is to identify the items to be offered in the benefits package to a sponsor. An event's benefits list may include

- Exclusivity in an area
- On-site banners/signs
- Name/logo inclusion in maps, flyers, brochures, posters, billboards
- On-site sampling
- PA announcement from stage
- Product display or sales
- Priority viewing/VIP seats for concert
- Priority parking
- Website exposure
- Cross promotions/tying sponsors together
- Street pole banners
- On-stage presence
- Radio exposure
- Television exposure
- Print exposure
- Hospitality tickets
- Entry in parade
- Ad in program book
- Ticket allocation and discount on additional tickets
- Merchandise discounts

After completing the event inventory and potential benefits listing, the next step is to organize these elements into levels of sponsorships to create a complete sponsorship package. When designing the sponsorship package, assign the most significant event elements and the best benefits to the highest priced sponsorship. Usually, the benefits presented in the lower level are also offered at the higher levels. The benefits expand as the sponsorship levels increase. The simplest method to price an event is to determine the value of each event component and then add the cost of the specific benefits. One must keep in mind that many components will have an intrinsic value rather than a fixed cost. The sponsorship costs should fluctuate appropriately to the offered benefits.

Once the different sponsorship levels have been determined, the next step is to decide how many sponsorships will be available at each level. Unlimited sponsors receiving the same package is not generally attractive to most businesses. Controlling the number of sponsorships in each level will optimize the benefit opportunities.

Types of Sponsors

There are many different levels and types of sponsors, so it is important to create unique sponsorship packages for each specific sponsor. Sponsors may fit more than one type and/or choose multiple packages to participate in more than one area or element of the event.

Title Sponsor. The sponsor has its name incorporated into the title of the event. This is an exclusive sponsorship and should be financially advantageous for the event. One must not give this sponsorship away too cheaply. It is also important to match a title sponsorship to the event goals and mission.

Presenting Sponsor. This sponsorship is one level below the title sponsor. Media sponsors tend to participate in this level. This sponsorship can be a secondary sponsor if the title sponsor has been sold or it can be the primary sponsor if there is no title sponsorship (e.g., Spring Fling presented by WXYZ Radio, Any Town Bank Arts Festival presented by the *Daily Times*). Also, this level can be the secondary sponsor for specific event elements (e.g., Sprint Stage presented by Pepsi).

Official Product Designation. This is an exclusive sponsorship to become the official soft drink, alcoholic beverage, automobile, credit card, cellular phone, long distance service, financial institution, or apparel of the event.

Area Sponsor. A strategy to obtain numerous large dollar sponsorships is to sell the title of each event area and component to a different sponsor (e.g., Gerber Childrenswear Kids' Korner).

Cosponsor. At this level, sponsors share both the level and the marketing exposure with one or more sponsors (e.g., Downtown Holiday Parade sponsored by Pepsi, America Bank and WABC-TV). Cosponsorships can occur at any level except for title sponsorship.

Media Sponsor. Media sponsors provide promotional support (usually in-kind) for the event in addition to making the sponsorship package worth more. After the media sponsor has committed to an agreed upon promotional package, the event can then pass this marketing value on to other sponsors. For example, secure the local newspaper as a presenting sponsor who would provide *x* amount of ad space to promote the event. Then in turn the event sells a co-sponsorship to ABC Cellular who would receive *x* amount of exposure in the local newspaper. At times media sponsors will donate cash; however, this is usually reserved for exceptional circumstances.

Keep in mind that radio stations are often great stage sponsors. They can contribute to the event by helping to book and/or promote the entertainment. The radio station can assist the event by compiling a list of potential performers that matches both the station's and event's target audiences; however, the event should maintain final authority over the selection of the entertainment. The station promotes their stage, thus promoting the event. Numerous stages at events can have different radio stations as sponsors. Additionally, the station's on-air personalities can serve as the MC for the stage.

In-Kind Sponsor. Many businesses are able to donate products or services rather than cash, which in turn helps to lower the event expenses. In-kind donations should be sought for all line item materials, supplies, personnel, and services needed for the event. Treat in-kind sponsors the same as cash sponsors by determining the value of the donation and thus establishing the appropriate sponsorship package.

Product Endorsement. This kind of sponsor pays for the personal appearance of a celebrity or famous spokesperson to appear at the event. While at the event the person endorses the sponsor's product or service, signs autographs, poses for photos, introduces entertainment, and so forth. This sponsor helps to draw spectators and media to the event.

Identifying Potential Sponsors

Companies have different reasons and needs when deciding whether to sponsor an event. Every company is not appropriate for every event. The process begins by creating a list of types of businesses that match the target market of the event. The company's products or services should also be considered when identifying potential sponsors for the events. For instance, for a concert series that attracts 20- to 30-year-olds, potential business categories may include apartment complexes, car dealerships, clubs and restaurants, stereo dealers, wireless phone companies, gyms, and banks. However, for a concert series that attracts 40- to 50-year-olds, the target categories could include cigar stores, golf courses, resort developments, wine distributors, men's clothing stores, and mortgage companies.

Every potential sponsor has distinct goals and objectives when sponsoring an event. Generic sponsorship packages should not be created and sent out to lists of businesses. By generating a package that includes all the sponsorship opportunities along with cost, specific sponsorship proposals can be created for designated businesses. Develop individual proposals for each potential sponsor with the composition of each package based on specialized objectives for each sponsor.

Before approaching a business regarding sponsorships, spend time to investigate potential businesses. The following information must be identified:

- Individual or department responsible for making sponsorship decisions
- Company history and reasons for contributing
- Previous sponsorships with this or other events
- Company requirements or specific forms for request
- Company's fiscal year
- Company's time frame for receiving and processing a request
- Company's target market
- Company's advertising history within the community
- Company's reputation within the community

Sponsorship Proposal

Once the sponsorship package has been developed, the next step is to create a sponsorship proposal for prospective sponsors. The success to selling sponsorships requires matching the event's sponsorship benefits and marketing package to an appropriate business. There is no one way to write a proposal. However, certain ingredients should be included in all proposals, such as

1. Executive Summary
   History of Event—How many years has the event been in operation?
   Event Background
   Event Goals
   Target Audience
   Past or Anticipated Attendance
2. Activities and Attractions Offered
3. Media Exposure and Marketing Efforts
4. Proposed Opportunity
   Benefits Package
   Cost and Payment Schedules
5. Deadline for Decision Agenda
6. Sponsorship Contract

Appendix 7.1 (p. 55) is an example of a sponsorship proposal for a weekly concert series.

Sponsor Sales Meeting

A personal visit with a prospective sponsor is one of the first opportunities for a sponsor to learn about the event and his or her potential role in the event. From research of the company, the event planner makes initial contact with the person within the company who has the authority to make sponsorship decisions. When making the initial call, briefly introduce the event and request an appointment with the potential sponsor to further discuss the event and the opportunities available.

Enter the sponsor meeting with a well-thought-out proposal, leaving room to customize the sponsorship (i.e., flexibility) the proposal to meet the needs of the sponsor. Be on time (or early)—running late may terminate the potential sponsorship. Ask an event board member to attend the sales meeting to emphasize the objectives of the event as well as show enthusiasm for the potential sponsorship.

Limit the initial meeting to 30 minutes, unless the situation indicates otherwise. Make a positive and brief presentation, explaining the need that the event serves in the community. Discuss the benefits associated with the sponsorship. Before leaving the meeting, discuss with the potential sponsor the next steps—when the event planner will follow-up to answer questions about the proposal as well as a target date for a decision. Be mindful that, unlike regular sales calls, sponsorships are rarely agreed upon at the initial meeting.

Sponsor Fulfillment

Creativity is key when compiling the sponsor hospitality package. When the benefits are delivered to the sponsor, their reaction should be, "Wow, this is great!" If possible, one should deliver more benefits than expected, especially for the loyal sponsors. If a specific area was not sold, it should be given to a sponsor as an extra bonus. This does not cost the event but will help to guarantee the sponsorship for the future.

Sponsors must receive everything that they were promised in the sponsorship package. Have a key person in charge of sponsorship fulfillment during the event. This person confirms that all banners, signs, and the on-site location is acceptable to the sponsor throughout the entire event. In addition, this person should be accessible to greet VIPs and act as a liaison on site.

Post-Event

Events should justify the sponsor's involvement by providing a post-evaluation of the event as a whole as well as the sponsorship. This requires feedback from the sponsor. Were the sponsor's goals and objectives of participation meet? Did the sponsor track sales before and during the event? Were the sales directly related to association with the event? Did event attendees sample the sponsor's product (i.e., increase awareness)? Was the sponsor's image increased in the community due to association with and marketing of the event? Theses answers should be answered and provided to the sponsor with a post-event evaluation that includes the following:

- Thank-you letter
- Event recap (including media coverage and values)
- Photos of their business logo in use during the event
- Photos of sponsor's on-site presence (e.g., booth, banners, employees)
- Illustration of other sponsorship benefits (e.g., example of the ticket with sponsor's name)
- Event evaluation
- Commemorative plaque, poster, or certificate
- Renewal suggestion for next year

This package is presented to the sponsor as soon as possible after the event. Finally, one should keep in touch with sponsors throughout the year and not just call on businesses when you need their money. One should also consider asking sponsors their opinion regarding changes in the event, new ideas or event components, fee or venue changes, and any change in the event vision and goals. It is easy to build a long-term relationship with sponsors, and they will feel important, appreciated, and a part of the event "family."

Appendix 7.1: Sponsorship Proposals for Weekly Concert Series (Alive After Five)

Event Information

Date and Time
Fridays, April 1–October 5, 20__
5:00p.m.–9:00p.m.

Location
City Plaza, downtown Anytown, USA

Event
Established as a fundraiser for the Local Arts Council and its umbrella organizations, *Alive After Five* is a traditional, weekly music series that attracts a consistent audience of young, downtown enthusiasts. Featuring live entertainment, *Alive After Five* integrates and promotes local art organizations to the general public, as well as creating a social scene for everyone in Anytown, USA.

Participants
Local and regional blues, rock, and easy listening talent.

Media and Marketing Efforts
Alive After Five will benefit from the promotional partnership with a well-known local radio station (WXXX 555.5FM). The general marketing schedule is designed to reach citizens of the Anytown who enjoy a safe and entertaining evening in our beautiful downtown. In addition, local marketing efforts will include print, television, and Internet exposure.

Funding
Corporate sponsorship and concession programs.

Admission
Free

Attendance
1,500 per week

Alive After Five Title Sponsor $25,000

The 27-week Title Sponsorship offers your company complete ownership of this popular event. *Alive After Five* will attract thousands of event guests to a safe and festive environment. Your company will benefit from this corporate branding opportunity, as your name will be integrated into the series title (*Company's Name Alive After Five*). Print media will offer your company extensive print impressions, while radio and PA announcements will offer thousands of additional audio impressions.

Corporate Recognition

Total Event Exclusivity
Allows your company to reach a target audience of more than 40,000 without competition.

Priority Banner Placement
Banner to be placed behind the stage for the duration of the Series. Banners to be provided by sponsor.

On-site Exposure
Opportunity to utilize 10-foot by 10-foot tent each week of the series. Tent provided by *Alive After Five*. Sponsor opportunity includes product sampling and/or coupon distribution.

Stage Announcements
Includes acknowledgment of your sponsorship and highlights your company's products.

Name/Logo Incorporated in Event Materials
Used in all event public communications materials including stationery, website, and press releases.

Television and Radio Exposure
Company name/logo represented in all radio and television promotional spots as title sponsor.

Print and Logo Exposure
Logo recognition on each event flier promoting the event. Priority logo placement on all *Alive After Five* print advertisements. Priority logo placement on event promotional poster.

Hospitality
Complimentary drink tickets for beer, wine, and soft drinks.

Total Sponsorship Value = *$XXX,XXX**

* The total sponsorship value is determined by adding the following estimates: the value of the total number of impressions, media value, and/or the value of on-site presence.

Alive After Five Series Sponsor $7,000

The 27-week Series Sponsorship offers your company exposure to thousands of event attendees the duration of the music series. *Alive After Five* will attract thousands of event guests to a safe and festive environment.

Corporate Recognition

Banner Placement
Placement of corporate banner each night of the event. Banners to be provided by sponsor.

On-site Exposure
Opportunity to utilize 10-foot by 10-foot tent each week of the series. Tent provided by *Alive After Five*. Sponsor opportunity includes product sampling and/or coupon distribution.

Stage Announcements
Includes acknowledgment of your sponsorship.

Radio Exposure
Company name represented in a limited number of radio promotional spots.

Print and Logo Exposure
Logo recognition on each event flier promoting the event. Logo placement on all *Alive After Five* print advertisements. Logo placement on event promotional poster.

Hospitality
Complimentary drink tickets for beer, wine, and soft drinks.

Total Sponsorship Value = *$XX,XXX*

Alive After Five Weekly Sponsor $400

The Weekly Sponsorship offers your company exposure to over one thousand event attendees as well as provides an opportunity to host clients and/or employees.

Corporate Recognition

Banner Placement
Placement of corporate banner on the night of your sponsorship. Banner to be provided by sponsor.

On-site Exposure
Opportunity to utilize 10-foot by 10-foot tent on the night of your sponsorship. Tent provided by *Alive After Five*. Sponsor opportunity includes product sampling and/or coupon distribution.

Stage Announcements
Includes acknowledgment of your sponsorship.

Radio Exposure
Company name represented in a limited number of radio promotional spots during the week of your sponsorship.

Print and Logo Exposure
Logo recognition in event print advertisement on the week of your sponsorship.

Hospitality
Complimentary drink tickets for beer, wine, and soft drinks.

Total Sponsorship Value = *$X,XXX*

Chapter 8
Risk Management

Developing a Comprehensive Risk Management Plan

Event planning is challenging enough without having to be concerned about things going wrong and who is at fault. However, risk management can be one of the most significant responsibilities for the event planner. All events have an element of risk, some higher than others. Event risk management means to safeguard people, property, reputations, and assets. It is the process of anticipating, preventing, or minimizing potential costs, losses, or problems for the event, organization, and guests.

Those involved in planning special events are obligated to operate according to the laws, codes, and regulations that pertain to them. This can include insurance and permit requirements, age limits, fire regulations, and health codes. An event manager should be familiar with the laws and local codes applying to their event and arrange to work with those involved to assure compliance. Local cooperation, acceptance, and support are key in running a successful event. Serious problems can arise if an event does not have the cooperation of local city officials, local police, and local fire departments.

Inadequate communications can pose huge problems for an event. At least three weeks prior to the event, hold a communications meeting with representatives from each city, county, and state departments (e.g., police, fire, health, traffic, sanitation, parks and recreation) who may be involved with the event. A written build-out sheet, a schedule of events, site map, road closure map, and task sheets should be the focus of the meeting.

Risk Analysis

The identification of risk factors must take place before an event and while there is plenty of time to do something about situations discovered. Because most events are set up on the day of the event, certain risk factors may not be identified until then. Therefore, it is essential to find out as much as possible prior to the event and to begin discussing plans with appropriate personnel and by constantly reviewing the various operational plans. Potential hazards and threats that may become risk factors at an event include

- Bad weather
- Dangerous equipment
- Overcrowding
- Inadequate management
- Ineffective alcohol control
- Poorly trained staff
- Terrorism
- Gang activity
- Food and water contamination
- Kidnapping

Can risk be completely eliminated? No. However, thorough and proper planning can reduce an event's risk. Event planners have a duty to engage in planning and prevention consistent with the requirements of any other industry. Event planners are responsible for having knowledge of safety standards and procedures, a means for self-evaluation, and constant innovation and improvement. All operational plans should be in writing and should specify who is responsible for which actions. Conducting a safe and secure event involves the actions of a number of people. One minor mistake may generate a more serious error. One broken promise or delay can create several others.

Event Safety and Security

The perception of a safe, secure event is critical to the success of the event and to its attractiveness as a destination. Security services should be on patrol from set-up to tear-down. Proper security will reduce the incidents of public disorder and criminal behavior.

Events can attract large crowds of people. As the number of people increases, so does the probability of accidents and crime. Events bring with them big responsibilities and potential liabilities. Security, health, and comfort problems are magnified greatly as the size of a crowd increases. Anticipate large crowds and what safety measures may be needed. Any build-up of energy from overcrowding is subject to a sudden release, which may impact people and property. Out of control energy can develop from excitement, frustration, anger, or racial tensions. Organizers must establish crowd control measures, such as regulating the use of skateboards and roller blades and forbidding running through the festival. One should create or strengthen barriers and distances that will reduce the likelihood of people being injured and property being damaged. Examples include

- Placement of barrier between the audience and the front of the entertainment stage

- Placement of vehicle barrier at least 20 feet from pedestrian traffic
- Placement of barrier to prevent vehicle and pedestrian traffic from flowing onto private property or environmentally sensitive areas

It is also important to eliminate items that can create hazards if crowds get unruly (e.g., glass bottles, cans).

Command Center

It is often advisable to have one central command post for an event. For large, multiday events, the command center should be operational 24 hours a day for the duration of the event. Many municipal jurisdictions will provide a mobile unit designed for this purpose. Emergency service personnel (e.g., fire, police, medical) should be placed within a strategic location for quicker and closer response time in an emergency. The purpose of the command center is

- To make all major safety and security decisions during an event.
- To centralize and coordinate security and emergency response.
- To allow for a unified exchange of information to resolve emergencies.

The following factors should be considered in choosing a location for the command center:

- Will a fire, riot, or any emergency make the command post inaccessible or inoperative? Can it be moved easily if necessary?
- Is adequate space and power available?
- Is the location accessible to other operations?
- Is the location removed enough from where crowds will congregate?
- Are phone lines available?

Vehicle and Pedestrian Control

Congested traffic is frustrating and dangerous for those attending the event as well as for citizens trying to get around the event. Organizers must anticipate any condition that can create traffic congestion. Also, one must keep in mind that pedestrians going to and from the event can create serious traffic conditions. It should be determined if additional equipment is necessary to facilitate the control of vehicular and pedestrian traffic, such as cones, barricades, traffic display boards, or signs.

Event planners must inform appropriate authorities in writing of the type of event, location, dates and times, and proposed road closures. This should include city, county, and state police; traffic, fire, and medical services; bus and transportation departments; bridge or tunnel authorities; local businesses; and trucking, shipping, and delivery companies. Jurisdictions vary on requirements regarding permit applications, time frame for application submission, public notification, and fees. An emergency plan for police, fire, and medical personnel must be created. One must not forget to include maps of the event area, road closure times and dates, and emergency response routes.

Parking is the place where first impressions are made. Determine the likelihood of illegal, spontaneous parking and how it can be addressed and prevented.

Nonsworn Security

Although some security guard companies now specialize in special events, many of their personnel are part-time with a high rate of turnover. Appropriate positions for nonsworn security include backstage security, VIP/patron access areas, and parking areas. Positions where nonsworn security would be inappropriate include traffic control, finance security, and cash collection.

Health and Food Service

When an event sells food and beverage or contracts with vendors to conduct these sales, several risk management concerns emerge. It is the event organization's responsibility and legal duty not to subject their attendees to unreasonable risk or harm. Areas where event organizers could be negligent include recruiting or retaining the food vendors and selecting the suppliers and food storage facility for the event. Event organizers can reduce the event's exposure of liability by

- Conducting a complete site inspection before and during the event
- Checking for fire safety and health hazards
- Conducting reference checks on all suppliers
- Getting certificates of insurance from all suppliers and vendors
- Having agreements signed by food service providers stating the company will comply with all health, safety, and fire regulations
- Having comprehensive general liability insurance.
- Having the health department inspect all food vendors on the site

It may be determined that there is negligence on behalf of the food service provider if

- The vendor could have been more prudent in preparing or serving the food.
- It is reasonable that the vendor ought to have recognized the food was spoiled or not stored appropriately.
- The vendor did not properly monitor the food.

Event Liability

General Liability

General liability insurance is a necessity for all events. It covers claims of bodily injury, property damage, and personal injury resulting from the event. Event organizers should determine the amount of liability insurance to purchase based on the type of event, requirements from local jurisdictions, and advice from an attorney. Most municipal jurisdictions require indemnification and hold harmless agreements with events. The indemnity clause transfers liability from the municipality to the event organizing body.

Shop around and shop early because event liability insurance can be difficult to obtain and price quotes and coverages vary dramatically between insurance carriers. Use insurance companies familiar with the event business. Share with insurance companies the events' risk management policies and also identify and provide event elements that may cause a need for additional insurance. Before purchasing, the event planner should compare policies, not just prices, to assure proper coverage for all possible risks. A certificate of insurance is a printed document authenticating proof of insurance, stating the amount of coverage, the dates and times the coverage is in effect, and who it covers.

Negligence from any event personnel can turn a certificate of insurance into an expensive piece of paper. Many times it does not matter if the event is actually negligent. The event organizers will have to prove there was no negligence. There is a legal duty of reasonable care, which means there is

- An obligation to examine all details of an event and act appropriately
- A responsibility to educate and inform participants and spectators of any potential hazards or conditions
- A responsibility to plan for the protection and safety of all participants and spectators
- A duty not to expose participants and spectators to unnecessary hazards

Liquor Liability

Event planners need to be aware of the "dram shop law," which in more than 40 states extends liability in the event of an incident due to excessive alcohol consumption to the hosts of an event serving alcohol. Because of the high liability with hosted events, most municipalities enforce rules and require liquor liability insurance to be carried by any event serving alcohol. The dram shop law indicates that the event liability is based on the selling of alcohol to someone either obviously intoxicated or underage.

To prevent injury (or death) to a third party and/or to avoid potential liability, event planners must exercise prudence and take affirmative steps to control the responsible service of alcohol to attendees. When an event is serving alcohol, proper serving precautions must be implemented. Examples of responsible service of alcohol may include

- Requiring one-ounce pour, not a free pour (if liquor drinks are permitted).
- Limiting the length of service, not extending the drinking beyond the designated time, and not announcing a last call for alcohol.
- Using only trained volunteers as bartenders. In addition, give them written instructions not to serve persons either underage or noticeably intoxicated.
- Initiating a control system to verify that minors and intoxicated persons are not served alcohol.
- Designating event staff to implement the system, supervising the bartenders, and intervening when necessary.
- Hiring security personnel to check IDs and monitoring minors.
- Displaying signs in visible locations to advocate responsible drinking by event attendees.
- Carrying an assortment of nonalcoholic drinks, and assuring bartenders are prompt to suggest them to attendees.
- Making sure there is plenty of food available for consumption.

Liability may also be transferred to the event if it is determined that there was an opportunity to keep a person from becoming intoxicated or from driving, but this did not happen. In addition, liability may also be transferred to the event personnel if they neglected to act when identifying or had the opportunity to identify an intoxicated event attendee as a foreseeable danger or at risk of injuring a third party. Three general mitigating circumstances determine social host liability:

1. Did the event supply and administer the sale of alcohol?
2. Was the event in a position to notice the condition of the intoxicated party?
3. Did the event have a responsibility to take prudent precautions to inhibit an intoxicated person from injuring a third party?

Americans With Disabilities Act

Enacted on July 26, 1990, the Americans with Disabilities Act (ADA) defines an individual with a disability as one who has a physical or mental impairment that substantially limits one or more "major life activities," such as walking, seeing, hearing, speaking, or taking care of oneself. This also applies to a person who has a record of such an impairment, or is regarded as having such an impairment. This includes contagious and noncontagious diseases; orthopedic, visual, speech, and hearing impairments; as well as cerebral palsy, epilepsy, muscular dystrophy, cancer, heart disease, diabetes, mental retardation, learning disabilities, HIV, drug addiction, and alcoholism. The ADA requires adaptations in policies, practices, and procedures, including

- Furnishing auxiliary aids when necessary to guarantee communication
- Displaying signs and information pertaining to provided special services
- Removing barriers
- Providing accessible parking sites
- Not assessing surcharges on those with a disability

When feasible, events should make obvious accommodations (e.g., reserved parking, reserved seating, and handicapped restrooms or portable toilets), unless making modifications would fundamentally alter the nature of the goods, services, and facilities. To become ADA compliant, event organizers should

- Become familiar with the needs of disabled individuals.
- Solicit the assistance of a disabled person to help identify needs.
- Take steps to conform with the law and to accommodate individuals.
- Conduct site inspections to identify potential barriers.
- Assign a staff member as on-site contact for questions, concerns or problems with accessibility.
- Advertise plans and special accommodations.

Crisis Management

Emergency preparedness must not be overlooked, waiting until a disaster prompts action. Every feasible problem cannot always be foreseen. However, a plan must be in place to deal with the unexpected or when disaster happens. One should create contingency plans and checklists with strategies to deal with potential and unanticipated occurrences. Event organizers should note the following risk situations within written emergency plans:

- Severe weather
- Extreme medical situations or death
- Riots
- Fires
- Gang activity
- Performance no-shows
- Excessive public drunkenness
- Electrical or equipment failure
- Emergency evacuation
- Vicious animals
- Terrorism
- Kidnapped children

One must identify the key personnel who need to be involved when a decision must be made regarding a crisis. Also, identify other parties who may need to be contacted during the emergency (e.g., city personnel, insurance agents, event attorneys). The crisis management plan must identify one person who is a final decision maker in all crisis situations.

Chapter 9
Operation Plan

The operation plan is the process of gathering all of the specific details required for the event. The event organizers must know what is needed for every element, component, and area for the event; where everything will go; and how specifics get in place.

Obtain Appropriate Permits

Individuals, organizations, and agencies wishing to conduct public events are usually required to obtain numerous permits in advance. Depending upon the state, municipality, and facility where the event is to be held, different regulations will be in place (e.g., event or parade permit, state and city alcohol permit, health permits, labor permit). Also, there may be additional local business licenses and/or permits needed.

Select Vendors

Many different types of food and beverage vendors can be selected to serve during events. Special attention should be placed on the event's goals and objectives before selecting concession vendors. One should remember to check with the local health department on regulations pertaining to outdoor food service.

Food and beverage menu items and prices can create a significant positive atmosphere within the event or, in contrast, initiate negative feedback. Will only full-service restaurants from the host community be allowed to be a part of the event? Will concession trailers be permitted?

Certain vendor information needs to be determined prior to the event, such as

- Vendor's power needs (i.e., amps, volts, and circuits)
- Other special needs (e.g., potable water, grease removal)
- Amount of set-up time
- Event entrance and parking location
- Parking location for stock truck
- Availability of ice and refrigeration storage

Event organizers must decide whether the vendors will pay a flat fee or a fee plus a percentage of their gross sales. Both methods have their merits depending on the type and size of the event. See Appendix 9.1 (p. 67) for an example of a food vendor application for a local food festival.

Entertainment

The decision to offer entertainment at an event can be complex and have huge implications on the event budget. Keep in mind that the cost of the talent is not the only cost consideration for the event budget. Most costs vary from production to production, depending on size of required stage, sound and lights, and venue specifications. Typical expenses associated with entertainment include venue rental, stage, sound and lights, security, catering, printing tickets, box office fees, advertising, hotel accommodations, transportation, and labor costs.

The type of entertainment should be based on the event's goals and objectives. When selecting appropriate entertainment for an event, the primary objective should appeal to interest of the target audience. Determine what type of music or performance will attract the appropriate audience for the specific event. After defining the type of performance, the appropriate artist selection can begin.

Booking Performers

Entertainment can be booked directly with the performer or through an entertainment agency. Advantages when using an agency include (1) they can offer a variety of acts, and (2) they provide information regarding specific performers, contracts, and riders. Entertainment agencies can also suggest appropriate options based on the event budget, target audience, and event venue.

Next, the event planner should obtain a list of available artists within the event's price range. Most artists have their own contract defining fees, terms of payments, technical requirements, cancellation policy, advertising requirements, accommodations and hospitality requirements, and more. Contract and fee negotiations can be effortless or extremely complicated. Make sure there is a complete understanding of the contract and all specified requirements, and be sure to carefully review the technical requirements and performance rider prior to signing the contract. Often, the contract can be simple while the rider is more complex and can add additional expenses for production, travel, and hospitality. If the contract is unclear, the booking agent should be asked in writing for further clarification. Appendix 9.2 (p. 70) offers an example of a sample contract for a concert series.

Music Licensing

Events with paid or unpaid entertainment must secure a music license from both American Society of Composers, Authors, and Publishers (ASCAP), and Broadcast Music Incorporated (BMI). Licensing is required when music is publicly performed, either live or recorded. Responsibility for any and all music played or performed at an event rests with the sponsoring organization of the event.

ASCAP and BMI combined hold licenses for 95% of music written and published in the United States. The fee for recorded music and live music is based on the number of people in attendance. To receive an exception for the license, all four of the following conditions must be met:

1. The music is not broadcasted or transmitted from the place at which it is performed.
2. There is no direct or indirect commercial interest associated to the performance.
3. There is no compensation for the performance by the performers, promoters, or organizers.
4. There is no admission fee, direct or indirect. However, there are exceptions for charitable, religious, and educational purposes.

Event planners unfamiliar with ASCAP and BMI licensing should consult with an attorney familiar with copyright law before signing entertainment contracts.

Determine Site Needs

Site Walk-Through

A site walk-through is extremely important and valuable. While walking through the site, look at possible conflicts between event components (e.g., stage vs. PA announcements, children's area vs. beer garden), between vendors and existing merchants (e.g., barbeque smoke vs. clothing stores), and between competing vendors. Also make note of the slope of the roads, parking lots, plazas, and grassy areas. What is the relationship of sun and the impact of shade on event areas? Are there any wind tunnels or a blockage of wind that may create problems? Are there business or resident access issues that may need to be addressed, such as banks, hotels, or doctors' offices?

If the event is going to take place a night, it is advisable to conduct at least one walk-through during the evening. Make note of areas that may need additional lighting, curbs that may be hard to see, sight lines, and so forth. The walk-through will help when creating the site layout, determining the site needs, and creating the timeline for site set-up.

Site Layout: Mapping the Site

After the site visit, the next step involves creating a scale drawing displaying all event areas, components, and fixtures. Display the event site within the facility site illustrating roads to be closed, parking facilities, concert stages, children's area, and so forth. While laying out the site, the planners should be aware of possible conflicts within the event site (e.g., beer booth beside children's activities) and conflicts between the event and the infrastructure (e.g., smoking barbeque tent in front of a clothing store). Usually the site map stays a work in progress up until the day of the event. The event site map should include

- Food vendor locations
- Beverages
- Sponsor locations
- Event headquarters
- Stages
- Children's area
- Lost-and-found area
- Ticket sales location
- Information booths
- First-aid location
- Volunteer check-in
- Volunteer and sponsor hospitality areas
- Restroom facilities
- Water for vendors and participants
- ATM machines
- Activity areas
- Finance headquarters
- Trash disposal sites
- Vendor, public, handicapped, sponsor, and volunteer parking
- Vendor stock truck area
- Electrical grids

Parking

The event planner must assess if there is adequate and available parking during the event. If inadequate parking is an issue, coordinating shuttle service from an outlying parking venue may be necessary. Considerations for parking may include

- Proper lighting—Is the lot well lit?
- Convenient to the event site
- Permits or fees involved
- Traffic flow into and out of the event site
- Parking area security

Electrical

Events with vendors, stages, and ancillary activities always require power. At times an event location will have permanent power sources; however, a majority of events need temporary power via power drops or generators. Determine early in the planning process all anticipated electrical needs. This involves not only knowing the amount of amperage required, but also determining the number of different circuits needed for each specific event component. To determine the amount of electricity needed, have all vendors and committees responsible for event areas to provide a list of specific items that will require electricity. Appendix 9.3 (p. 71) provides an example of an electrical needs form.

Contract with a qualified electrician to review the power requirements and assist in the laying out the event site. The event electrician is often one of the most important links between the event and its vendors. An electrical failure can bring the event to a halt. It is essential and worth the expense to have an electrician on-site to handle and correct any problems as quickly as they occur for the event to continue.

If using generators, be aware of possible noise and fumes. Invest newer, quieter generators. Consult the electrician about the type of generators needed.

Communications

Adequate and dependable communications equipment is critical to running a smooth event. Renting radios, walkie-talkies, or other similar devices (e.g., cell phones, two-way phones) is necessary for key personnel to stay in contact for both essential and nonessential details. A portable source of communication is a must to address situations as they occur. It is helpful to assign different event committees to specific channels to cut down on channel traffic and frustration of event personnel trying to get a clear channel. It helps to have separate channels for volunteers, event headquarters, the electrician, entertainment, vendors, emergency first aid, and security. Have key personnel carry cellular phones along with a list of numbers on a small laminated card.

Sanitation

Trash receptacles should be plentiful and easy to find and use. If the cans have lids or tops make sure they are open during the event. Rolling plastic containers are superior to cardboard containers for events lasting over several days. During larger events it helps to keep a trash compactor truck immediately off-site to empty receptacles during the event. Placement of this truck should be downhill from the event, and far enough away that sights and smells do not affect event patrons. Some event planners pay community groups, such as the Boy Scouts, $1 a cart to haul the containers to the truck for emptying.

Portable toilets should also be plentiful and always well-stocked with toilet paper. Planners should not forget handicap accessible toilets. Place sufficient toilets within close proximity of children's areas, stages, and beer locations. When placing toilets keep in mind adjacent businesses or other sensitive areas.

Signage

The event planner must print the necessary signs for directions, information, and various event costs to inform event attendees. Nothing can frustrate a festival-goer as much as being lost or not being able to find his or her way. Without proper signs throughout the festival, attendees may get frustrated and leave. Prepare professional looking signs and banners (with arrows) that are legible and easy to read and install them in visible places. Large maps that show specific areas and event components should be placed throughout the festival (e.g., at information booths). Examples of event signs include

- Ticket booths and prices
- Entertainment schedules
- First aid
- Information
- Food menus
- Alcohol and event policies
- Restrooms
- Sponsor recognition
- Parking
- Ancillary events
- Special areas
- Merchandise sales
- Admission prices/fees
- Lost children

Event Headquarters

An event headquarters should be established and manned throughout the event to centralize communication and emergency response. A member of the event planning team and a law enforcement representative should be present at all times while the event is open. The event headquarters notebook should be compiled prior to the event and include

- Emergency contact numbers (e.g., law enforcement officer in charge of event security, city or municipal contact person, fire marshal, health department representative, traffic, parking, electrician, ice or refrigerator truck, insurance representative, event

board members and steering committee members, stage company, booking agent)
- Severe weather plan
- Maps of facilities and site
- Schedule of event activities
- Copies of all agreements and contracts
- Permits and licenses
- Certificates of insurance
- Copies of alcohol permits (check dates and times)
- Inspection reports (e.g., fire, health, and building codes)
- Security plans
- Prepared press releases

It is important to set up the event headquarters a day or two prior to the start of the event. Headquarter tasks prior to the event include

- Make equipment check-out forms.
- Create a contact list with phone/pager numbers of all pertinent people.
- Make list of who receives an event radio, golf cart, and other equipment.
- Pack office supplies, staples, paper, markers, tape, and so forth.
- Create quick reference price sheets for beverages, concert tickets, merchandise, and other items being sold.
- Number and label all equipment.

Event Evaluation

Once the event is over and the site is torn down and cleaned up, a site inspection needs to occur. Return all event supplies (e.g., banners, site equipment). Finally it is time to evaluate the event. The planning committee should meet to discuss what went right or wrong, what could have been done better, what worked, and what did not work. Take written notes of all information, both good and bad, to be used when planning next year's event. The following questions should be asked and discussed:

- Were there sufficient staff and volunteers?
- Did the event meet the organization's goals?
- Was the event financially stable? (Complete a financial statement.)
- Are changes and/or additions necessary for next year's event?
- What were the results of the impact studies (e.g., visitors, economic, and social)?
- What suggestions came from sponsors and volunteers?
- What were the event's strengths and weaknesses?
- What areas need to be improved?
- What should be repeated and why?
- What were the favorite activities for festival guests and sponsors?
- Was there special media coverage?

Finally, planners should write thank-you notes to all who participated, sponsored the event, and volunteered in the planning process or during the event. Often events host a post-event appreciation party. A thank-you certificate or plaque is a wonderful way to show appreciation for someone's hard work and support.

Appendix 9.1: Food Vendor Application

Deadline: *Month, Date, 20__*

Official Use Only
Date Rec'vd ______
Amt Dep Paid _____
Chk# ____________
Accpt ____________

Submit to: *Downtown Events*
Food Vendor Coordinator
100 Main Street
Anytown, USA 12345

Please print the following information.

Restaurant Name: ____

Physical Restaurant Address: ____

City: ______________________________ State: ____________ Zip: ____________

Mailing Address: ____

City: ______________________________ State: ____________ Zip: ____________

Owner: ____

Contact Person for *Event Name*: ____

Restaurant Phone: ______________ Fax: ______________ Mobile: ______________

The standard fee includes one 14-foot by 14-foot tent and four 6-foot tables. Any additional space, power or tents will cost an additional fee. All tents will be provided by *Event Name*. ***Restaurants are not allowed to bring their own tent or trailer***. Restaurants will be permitted to bring in a trailer to unload supplies/equipment if needed.

Entry Fees

Standard Fee:	One 14-foot by 14-foot tent and four 6-foot tables	$400.00
Additional Items:	14-foot by 14-foot tent and four 6-foot tables	$300.00
	10-foot by 10-foot tent (no extra tables)	$100.00
	10-foot by 20-foot café space (no extra tables)	$50.00
	Electrical Charges	$________
	Total	$________

Please limit additional space request to one selection. For example, you may request ONE additional 14-foot by 14-foot tent or ONE additional 10-foot by 10-foot tent or ONE additional 10-foot by 20-foot café space. Due to space limitations, only a limited number of café areas will be provided. The café area will be located next to your regular tent. Restaurants responsible for providing their own tables, chairs, clean-up, and other supplies/services for their café area.

The standard fee includes set-up and breakdown of tent, tables, use of a refrigerated truck on-site, and trash can/trash pick-up. There are additional fees for electricity. Please note that *Event Name* does not provide chairs, extension cords, lighting, etc. ***Very Important***: *Event Name* requires each restaurant to bring and keep a fire extinguisher at its booth throughout the festival.

Electrical

Vendors needing electrical hook-ups will incur the following charges:

110v/20amp	$100.00 per plug in
220v/50amps or less	$175.00 per plug in
220v/51amps to 220v/100amps	$200.00 per plug in

Event Name has limitations and/or restrictions as to the electrical available. All electrical requests must be made by *Month Day, 20__*. Last minute electrical requests may not be honored.

Tickets

Event Name will pay each vendor an amount equal to 78% of the value of the tickets turned in during the *Event Name*. *Event Name* will retain 22% of the gross ticket amount. *Event Name* will remit to the Vendor his/her 78 percent of gross sales no later than 10 working days after the close of the event. Vendors will deliver tickets to a designated location where tickets will be weighed and/or counted. A Vendor representative must be present when the weigh-in takes place. A receipt will be issued to each party at the time of the weigh-in. ANY CONCERNS REGARDING TICKET WEIGH-IN MUST BE VOICED AT THE TIME OF THE WEIGH-IN/COUNT.

There is a five-ticket maximum for each food item sold by Vendors. No cash transactions will be allowed. Violators will be asked to leave the festival.

Menu and Vendor Selection

The *Event Name* Food Committee will review all menus to limit duplication among participants. Only three Vendors will be allowed to serve the same menu items. In addition, a maximum of five menu items (including drinks) is allowed per Vendor. First priority will be *Anytown* full-service restaurants. Beverages sold must be an item on the regular menu of the restaurant and produced at the restaurant, such as homemade iced tea, coffee, homemade lemonade, milk shakes or similar beverages. Sodas, water, sport drinks, fruit juices, alcohol of any kind, canned and bottled beverages or other brand name/commercial beverages may **not** be sold by participating *Event Name* restaurants. Only the items listed on this application may be sold. There is a five-ticket maximum per food item, which allows Vendors to serve tastes of their product. This provides festival guests an opportunity to visit more booths. Item descriptions and portion sizes must be listed. Applications that do not include this information will be considered incomplete.

Ice/Refrigeration

Ice will be sold on site throughout the event to participating Vendors at $3 per 25-pound bag. Bags of ice that Vendors use/request during the event will be tabulated and then deducted from the Vendor's ticket sales. If preferred, Vendors may go to the ice truck and pay for their ice with cash.

A secured refrigerated truck will be available on site and is available to Vendors for product storage. It is highly advised that Vendors distinctly label their product containers.

Each restaurant will be allowed to bring their own banner promoting their restaurant establishment only. Other names or sponsors will not be allowed on the banner. *Event Name* will provide each Vendor with a printed menu that will include the Vendor's name, items for sale, and ticket amounts.

All menu items and food preparation must comply with health department regulations. Used cooking oil/grease shall be disposed of in a manner approved by the health department (grease traps are available). Restaurants are encouraged to bring their own potable (drinkable) water to the festival since on-site potable water will be limited in its availability.

Item	**Description**	**Portion**	**# Tickets**
____________	______________________	________________	________
____________	______________________	________________	________
____________	______________________	________________	________
____________	______________________	________________	________
____________	______________________	________________	________

Insurance/Taxes
Vendors must supply *Event Name* with a certificate of general liability insurance by *Month, Date, 20__*. Any Vendor not supplying this document by this date will not be permitted to participate in the event. Coverage must be at least $1,000,000 general aggregate and $500,000 each occurrence. Vendors are also responsible for complying with local and state tax regulations.

Deadline Information
Registration deadline is *Day, Month Date, 20__*. Restaurants will be selected by *Month, Date Year*. Notification of Acceptance letters will be sent by *Month Date, 20__*.

****IMPORTANT—PLEASE READ****

Once your application has been accepted, restaurants are required to submit a current copy of their business license, liability insurance, and payment (if applicable).

I. The Restaurant/Vendor understands and agrees that there is no entitlement to any certain location in the festival and agrees and grants *Event Name* or its agent the full discretion regarding location at the *Event Name* festival.

II. Upon signing below, the Restaurant/Vendor agrees, understands, and acknowledges that *Event Name* does not and cannot guarantee the turn-out, the volume of sales, the weather conditions or the success of any Vendor or the festival. Accordingly, Restaurant/Vendor specifically agrees that it will hold harmless *Event Name* for any and all damages or losses that may occur as a result of festival participation by the by the Restaurant/Vendor. Specifically, Restaurant/Vendor understands and appreciates that there are inherent risks involved in festival participation and agrees to accept the risk of loss occasioned by participation in *Event Name*.

III. Restaurant/Vendor understands and agrees that space in *Event Name* is limited and submission of an application does not guarantee acceptance into *Event Name*. Moreover, once *Event Name* accepts an application and notifies Restaurant/Vendor of acceptance into *Event Name* festival, all fees become nonrefundable.

IV. If any provision of this agreement shall be held void, voidable, invalid, or inoperative no other provision of this agreement shall be affected as a result thereof, and accordingly, the remaining provisions of this agreement shall remain in full force and effect as though such void, voidable, invalid, or inoperative provision had not been contained herein.

V. In the event of a breach of this agreement by Restaurant/Vendor, *Event Name* shall be entitled to recover from Restaurant/Vendor its attorneys' fees in connection there with in addition to the costs of any action, suit, or proceeding.

VI. Except as otherwise provided in this agreement, all rights and remedies herein or otherwise shall be cumulative and none of them shall be in limitation of any other right or remedy.

VII. This agreement shall be governed by the laws of the state of *Anystate*.

VIII. This agreement sets forth the entire understanding of the parties hereto relating to the subject matter hereof. No modification, amendment, waiver, termination or discharge of this contract or of any of the terms or provision hereof shall be binding upon any of the parties hereto unless confirmed by a written instrument signed by authorized agents of the Restaurant/Vendor and *Event Name*. No waiver by either party of any term or provision of this contract or of any default hereunder shall affect the respective rights thereafter to enforce such term or provision or to exercise any right or remedy in the event of any other default, whether similar or not.

IX. It is agreed that all rules and regulations attached to this agreement are a part thereof and that no agreement other than those contained herein shall be binding upon the parties unless in writing and signed by an official of *Event Name*.

By this agreement duly signed, ____ agrees to abide by the conditions contained herein and officially confirms its participation in the *20__ Event Name*.

Signature: ____ Date: __________________________

Appendix 9.2: Performance Contract for Weekly Concert Series

Alive Downtown Performance Agreement

The following is a performance agreement between Alive Downtown and ____________________ (Band Name) for performance at Alive Downtown.

As a contracted performer for Alive Downtown, I/We hereby agree to the following terms:

Arrival/Set-up at the Event

A. Band will arrive on-site at the *name of location* no later than 4:00 p.m. on the day of the performance.
B. All equipment will be set-up and sound checks will be completed by 5:00 p.m.
C. Alive Downtown will provide all required sound equipment for performance, unless prior arrangements have been made with the Alive Downtown manager (not less that two weeks prior to scheduled performance).

Sets

A. Set 1: 5:15 p.m. – 6:00 p.m.
B. Set 2: 6:15 p.m. – 7:00 p.m.
C. Set 3: 7:15 p.m. – 8:00 p.m.

Payment

A. Band will receive payment of $__________, in the form of a check, following completion of the last set. NO CASH PAYMENTS WILL BE MADE.
B. Band will not receive payment if Alive Downtown is canceled 24 hours in advance of scheduled performance.
C. Band will receive 50% payment if Alive Downtown is canceled before 3:00 p.m. on day of event.
D. Bands not set up and ready to play by 5:15 p.m. and/or not playing all required sets will be assessed a $50 penalty. IN WHICH CASE, PAYMENT WILL BE MAILED THE FOLLOWING DAY.
E. Alive Downtown reserves the right to alter performance schedules as necessary.
F. W-9 information must be supplied before payment can be made.
G. Band must complete and return all material to the Alive Downtown event manager.

General Information (Please print clearly)

Performance Date: ____________________ Check Payable to: ____________________

Band Name: ____________________ Contact: ____________________

Address: ____
City State Zip

Phone/ Fax: ____________________ Mobile or Pager: ____________________

Signature: ____ Date: ____________
(Band Representative)

Signature: ____ Date: ____________
(Executive Director, Alive Downtown)

Appendix 9.3: Vendor Electrical Needs

One 110-volt, 20-amp single-plug outlet will be provided to each Vendor. However, please note that there will be a charge of $100 each for any additional 110v outlets (for amperage that exceeds 20 amps) and a charge of $150 each for any 208v or 220v outlets under 30 amps. No 208v or 220v outlets over 30 amps will be available. Power requirements need to be as specific as possible as they may determine a Vendor's on-site location.

Please indicate any additional electrical needs.

$ _____ Please provide me with ____ additional 110v outlets $100 each

$ _____ Please provide me with ____ 208v outlets $175 each

$ _____ Please provide me with ____ 220v outlets $200 each

$ _____ TOTAL AMOUNT DUE

Vendors must list all electrical equipment (e.g., lights, ranges, freezers, microwaves, stoves) with the appropriate amperage for each piece. Amperage information can be found on the back of most appliances. ***Applications that do not contain the following information will not be considered***. Amperage requirements will determine Vendor's on-site location.

Equipment Item	Amperage

Chapter 10
Event Ideas—Special Events and Community Celebrations

This is an assortment of event ideas for every budget. Quick tips and idea generators can be customized to fit your organization and event needs. These can be used to compliment existing events or start a new community tradition. Also included are examples of event competition rules, guidelines and forms.

A Day in the Park

Adventure Club—This is a great way to introduce children to outdoor activities. Participants learn basic skills and safety in shelter construction, survival, hiking, fishing, camping, and outdoor cooking. This activity may include an overnight camp-out.

Art in the Park—A beginner painting class for adults or children is offered. Participants will learn basic techniques using flora and fauna of the park as subjects.

Bark in the Park/Canine Festival/Dog Days of Summer/Wagging and Walking in the Park—Everyone come walk, waddle and wag! This is a canine carnival of activities for the animal lover. It is a great idea to obtain sponsorships from dog food companies, dog clubs, local vets, and dog product companies. Don't forget to invite organizations that represent wildlife, nature preserves, exotic animals, and pet healthcare experts to offer advice and tips regarding owning a pet. One may want to offer a pooch parade, dog costume/beauty contest, amazing animal tricks, unique acts or stunts, and pet art/paw prints. In addition to the activities, a showcase of animal products, services, and informative seminars may be included.

This entire day, centered around man's best friend, includes a *Canine Freestyle Dance Competition*, animal rescue training demonstrations, Police K-9 demonstrations, flyball tournaments, and canine presentations with demonstrations on obedience, herding, agility, and lure coursing.

Pets in all shapes and sizes join in the *Pooch/Pet Parade*, a pledge walk for animals. Owners put their best paw forward by collecting pledges to raise funds for their furry friends.

Spectators may be treated to a *Dog Costume/Beauty Contest* with categories such as a pet/owner look-alike contest, largest/smallest dog, most hair, least hair, best bark, longest ears, best-dressed dog, cutest pound puppy, homeliest dog, saddest eyes, and best of show. As an additional fundraiser, *Mutt and Mug Shots* (professional photos with man's best friend) may be offered. A *Celebrity Dog Wash* (radio, TV, and political personalities wash your best friend for a donation to the animal shelter) can be a doggone fun time.

All dogs must have current vaccinations. Assign someone to monitor the heat from any asphalt to prevent pets from burning their paws. Make sure to provide plenty of shade and water. Don't forget small swimming pools to wash the dogs, poop scoops, shampoo, tables, chairs, trash cans, towels, plastic aprons, straw, water hose, nozzles, nail clippers, and plenty of water bowls.

Catch a Trout—Local outfitter or fish shop sponsors a fishing booth complete with fly-fishing lessons. Local fish hatchery stocks "pool" with live trout. Proceeds go to local Trout Unlimited or similar charity.

Chalk the Park—Kids of all ages express themselves by making colorful chalk drawings throughout the park on the paths during the local arts festival.

Creatures of the Night—When night falls, a different world comes alive. Learn how nocturnal animals carry out their lives in a world of darkness.

Early Bird Breakfast—Participants rise and shine and enjoy breakfast while learning about proper equipment and techniques to identify local birds. Participants bring their own binoculars and bird checklist and discover how to attract birds to their own yards, and actually make feeders to take home.

Feathered Friends—Participants learn roles of raptors in nature's food web. Participants are given a chance to learn about the importance of hawks, vultures, falcons, owls, and eagles.

Fire, Stone, Hides, and Bone: Survival Skills From the Stone Age—Participants will be instructed in fire making, natural cordage, primitive weapons and tools made from stone and/or bone, and natural hide tanning.

Fishing and Wishing—Everyone can learn where, when, and how to catch a fish with techniques on how to bait a hook, and cast a line. If someone is lucky they may hook the big one. This is an exciting event element sure to be a "reel" hit.

Growing Organic Herbs—Teach participants to plant, grow, and care for their own fresh herbs.

Hints From Prints—Study local animals, their tracks, and habits. Participants also learn to make plaster casts.

Interpretive Scavenger Hunt—Hold an old-fashioned scavenger hunt in the great outdoors, in which participants look for a butterfly, insect, seed, vine, bark, male pinecone, female pinecone, needle, moss, and 10 different colors. They may also look for something smooth, smelly, sharp, that can make music, with five natural sides, and rough.

Let's Go Batty—Participants learn the best way to control mosquitoes around their house. Bats are nature's bug zappers. Participants learn all about these predators of the insect world and build a bat box to take home.

Life in the Dark—Participants come to check out the thousands of beautiful animals that prefer light of a different wavelength. General insect biology and the use of ultraviolet light to attract moths, beetles, and many other six-legged wonders of the night will be discussed.

"Lost" in Anytown USA—This is a spinoff of the TV reality series, in which participants find their way using a series of clues and challenges on an outdoor adventure hunt. Here's a map, here's a compass—everyone follows the checkpoints on the map in the order listed. Quickest time wins awards and prizes donated by local outfitter. It is a great way to get people out to see the sights that they may not be aware of and enjoy the out-of-doors.

Moonlight Canoe Float—Invite participants to go on a canoe ride at night with a full moon. New experiences, sights, and sounds will offer a magical evening.

Nature Photography Workshop—Participants gain valuable insights into proper equipment and techniques used for nature photography.

Nature of the River—Participants journey down to the local river and discover the plants and animals that make the river their home. The importance of the river over the centuries, not only to wildlife but also to man, is discussed. The program can be conducted from canoes or on the riverbank. Participants should bring a waterproof container, binoculars, and field guides.

Outdoor Gourmet—Introduce participants to the basics of outdoor stoves, meal planning, and cooking tips for the outdoor connoisseur. All menus are easy to prepare and pack. Taste testing included!

Plant and Flower Festivals—One can highlight his/her area's favorite plant or flower (e.g., iris, rose, tulips) with a festival that features the color and beauty of the natural landscape. The festival can illustrate the varieties and accessories for the plants and flowers. Include craft vendors, a horticulturist, and strolling musicians. Encourage festival-goers to bring their picnics to enjoy the park/garden for a full day of fun.

River Sweep, Beach Sweep—Participants take part in a national campaign to clean up rivers, lakes and beaches. Encourage everyone to wear boots and gloves and to come prepared to get dirty. It is important to provide garbage bags and a truck to haul the debris away.

Seed, Bulb, and Plant Exchange—Participants gather their extra seeds, bulbs, plants, or other garden materials to swap with fellow gardeners. They exchange their goodies for new and different surprises.

Sensing the World at Night—In this fun adventure of awareness participants experience the world of nature at night by utilizing all of the senses except one—sight. Everyone will be blindfolded on this safe hike and follow the group along a trail designed to heighten the senses during this exhilarating learning adventure.

Shakespeare in the Park/Playhouse in the Park—Present a selection of theater classics free to the public by securing the help of a local theater, high school group, or college students to produce a summer Shakespeare festival. Encourage spectators to bring picnics and blankets. A unique spin is to get the director to put a new twist on the old themes, such as presenting the plays in modern day context; however, the language remains classic English. One idea is to offer Shakespeare's *The Two Gentlemen of Verona* to be performed entirely in beachwear or the dark play of *Macbeth* in more modern Seattle grunge. The goal is to educate as well as entertain.

Spring Garden Tour—One can show off the local park and garden with guided tours describing planted annuals, perennials, and native trees.

The World After Dark/Owl Prowl/ Hootin' and Hollerin'—When the sun goes down, the big-eyed creatures of the moon and stars come out. Participants explore the creatures of the night. Fill the evening with stories of the night owls who screech and hoot. Discussions include topics about birds, mammals, insects, and reptiles. Include a stroll through the night woods to discover the mysteries of the darkness.

There's Something Fishy Here!—This fly fishing seminar offers an informative look at fly fishing, trout management, and conservation practices. There will be equipment displays and casting demonstrations. Local fishing guides discuss the uses of proper equipment and various techniques used to catch the trophy trout and bass. Participants learn the art of tying basic fly patterns and which flies to use under certain conditions.

Tiptoe Through the Tombstones—Take participants on a historic stroll through your oldest cemetery and discover what it can teach us.

Tree Give Away for Arbor Day—Give local residents small saplings to commemorate Arbor Day.

Twilight Boat Float—The diversity of aquatic life is observed during one of the most fascinating times of the day—twilight.

What on Earth Can I Do?—Celebrate Earth Day with lectures and demonstrations on recycling, composting, and endangered animals. Offer workshops on environmentally friendly or "green" products for consumers and review the three *R*s: reduce, recycle, reuse.

Where Are All the Wild Flowers?—Participants stroll through the local park spotting the native species of the many wild flowers in the area.

Arts Alive

Art Attack Fun Run—A 1K or 5K fun run may be added to kick off your arts festival.

Art in Action—In this high energy art participants construct large-scale and small-scale projects made from a variety of colorful materials.

Art in the Park/Spring Into the Arts—Feature local and regional visual artisans in an outdoor art show in the park. Participants watch and visit with artists as they demonstrate their amazing talent and creativity in a variety of media, including basketweaving, woodcarving, and pottery making.

Arti Gras—A celebration including music, drama, floats, mimes, and visual arts.

Champagne Stroll—A new idea to draw attention to the purchasing of original art. A wine distributor provides champagne for each art vendor or exhibiting artists purchase bottled wine and souvenir wine glasses from the festival. When someone purchases art, the vendor gives the patron a glass of champagne.

Children's Mask Making—Kids learn how to make a plaster mask of their face, and then everyone paints their mask to express who they are or what they want to be when they grow up.

***Community Wall Mural*—**A festival wall mural is a wonderful community project and can make an ordinary street or area into an extraordinary setting. It can be a great decorative cover for an otherwise ugly building, fence, or area. Construct out of wood, paper, or fabric. A local artist sketches a design that matches the festival theme or a significant community site. Involve high school art students to provide supervision and help prevent vandalism.

Creation Station/Discovery Tent/Imagination Station/ Imagine That!—Children try their hand at artistic expression with the help of local high school art students. These free hands-on arts and craft projects and activities are for children to experience and explore (e.g., T-shirt art, wearable art). A critter may be created from recycled materials. Area includes storytelling and interactive music. Creation with clay is always a hit with children.

Giant Weaving Project—Provide a hands-on experience to help participants develop an appreciation of making art. Solicit the help of a local weaver to create a simple loom using scaffolding, ladders, and ropes. Participants use old clothes and donated cloth as weaving material while creating a unique piece of art that will be displayed throughout the art show or festival.

Ice Cream Fundraiser—A wonderful way to raise money for the local arts council. Area artists donate handcrafted bowls to be "sold" ($10 donation) with two scoops of ice cream at the community art festival. It is a good idea to ask a local grocery store or ice cream vendor about sponsoring this event by donating the ice cream.

Paint by Number—Local artists or college students draw a canvas to be colored by festival-goers. A different theme is used each year, such as 25 most recognizable people/political figures of the community, festival posters, or scenes of the festival site. Place cups, each with a number, filled with washable latex paint by each section of the canvas. Use small brushes for better accuracy. The mural can be exhibited downtown or at a local mall after the event.

Paint Your Palate—Every event has to offer food of some sort, even the art festival. One should give the food court area a name that reflects the event while also selecting food vendors that not only feed the hungry, but also tantalize their taste buds.

Pee Wee Picasso—This children's art area offers the opportunity to create simple craft projects to take home. Participants have fun and use their imagination to create their own interpretation of a favorite painting.

***Sculpture in Public Places*—**Place sculpture exhibitions throughout the community, with a focus on the downtown local parks and major entrances into the community. Using high-traffic areas will allow thousands of viewers in the area to observe this artwork. *Sculpture in Public Places* is organized by the local municipality with the help of the state museum, state and local art commissions, area chamber of commerce, and donations from local businesses.

Cultural, Ethnic, and Heritage

Celebrating cultural diversity has grown in popularity, with many communities showcasing their ethnic differences through food, art, entertainment, and music. Observances of times past can present a community with tantalizing experiences, which function as both educational and entertaining.

African American Cultural Festival/ Roots and Heritage Festival—The community's cultural awareness of African and Caribbean history can be increased with live performances of drummers and dancers in authentic attire that illustrates the vibrancy indigenous to African culture. Offer dance seminars with audience participation and invite an African chief, witch doctor, and authentic storytellers. The storytelling program begins with a history of African story-telling and then a sample of interesting stories. The African marketplace can feature handmade arts and crafts and display artifacts of African culture such as baskets, clothing, and jewelry.

Black History—This may include storytelling and movies of famous people and episodes in Black History. A *Black History Poster Contest* with a theme such as "The Long Journey" is included so that everyone can get involved. One should invite local Black seniors to do an oral history of their life and ask them to bring old photographs, books, clothes, and artifacts to create a heritage display.

Bon Festival—This Japanese Festival features authentic music, food, dances, and displays.

Cajun Festival/Bayou Boogaloo—Turn up the heat with the hottest and spiciest weekend of the year! Festivities include live zydeco music and a crawfish cooking contest. Festival-goers feast on Cajun delicacies, such as steamed crawfish, jambalaya, gumbo, and a variety of other Creole dishes. Everyone comes to learn the basics and ingenious use of spices associated with the early Acadian settlers of Louisiana.

Cemetery Historic Tour—Take a walking tour in the local cemetery to highlight the history of the community. Tours can be self-guided with a booklet and map or led by a member of the local historic society.

Cinco de Mayo—Everyone celebrates the Mexican victory over the French at the Battle of Pueblo on May 5, 1862 by hosting a Cinco de Mayo celebration to observe Mexican pride and determination. The festivities may include sounds of mariachi, conjunto, or Tejano music, Tex-Mex foods, pinatas, folklorico dancing, low-rider contest, or any ethnically oriented family activities. A *Jalapeño Eating Contest* may be added for extra flare.

Cowboy Folk Festival—How exciting to bring the country to the city street with a street festival that would make a wrangler proud. One can serve barbecue and host a best rib competition, a best sauce competition, or a chili cook-off. Musical entertainment, featuring country bands and western swing music with added attractions such as line dancing and cowboy poets, should be provided. Participants can "pan for gold," rope a steer, or watch trick ropers in action.

Founders Festival—Festival-goers celebrate the founders of the community by offering activities and crafts. Quilting, needlework, and woodcarving can be just a few activities to be offered. Feature a tractor parade and an antique equipment exhibit. Include demonstrations and hands-on activities.

Hands Around the World/It's a Small World—Kids get an international flavor while attending the festival. Each child receives a passport when they enter the area. Then at each stop, they get the passports stamped. The children "travel" to different regions of the world and make craft souvenirs, such as boomerangs and aboriginal cave paintings at the Australian station. One should include an International Stage to entertain the children, involve a native dance, or have children participate in a pinata breaking party.

Harvest Festival/Heritage Day—Provide visitors with an opportunity to experience the 19th century during this fall time festival. Participants celebrate the agricultural era with activities and demonstrations, such as weaving, spinning, quilting, blacksmithing, butter-churning, cider pressing, candle dipping, pie-making contests, and hayrides. Invite participants to display old farm tools, machinery, and tractors.

Mardi Gras—Mardi Gras, or Fat Tuesday, is the last day of a carnival season that ends just before Lent. Key elements for any Mardi Gras include carnivals, spectacular parades with traditional bead-throwing, masquerade balls with the crowning of the Mardi Gras King and Queen, Cajun and zydeco music, street dances with costumes, and the use of the official Mardi Gras colors: purple, green, and gold.

Old Fashion Sunday/Tom Sawyer Days/Frontier Days—This is a day in the park reminiscent of the 1890s. One builds an Old Settlers Village with demonstrations of early pioneer activities, such as woodcarving, basket-weaving, butter-churning, candle-dipping, corn-grinding, and quilting. It is fun to offer entertainment that contains foot stomping, folk music, jug band instruments, square dancing, and clogging. Kids can play old-time games such as hoop rolling, dropping a clothespin in a bottle, frog hopping, sack races, and fence painting. (*Note*: National Tom Sawyer Day is July 4.)

One must not forget homemade ice cream, arts and crafts, watermelon seed spitting contest, pie baking contest, hog-calling, cake walks, wagon rides, and a display of antique cars and farm equipment. A great highlight to the day could be *Cow Patty Bingo*, where a pasture or field is divided into a grid of squares and each square "rents" for $5. The participant who purchased the square where Miss Bessie does her business wins a grand prize.

Renaissance Festival—Jousting, knights in armor, and lots of food adds to authentic period demonstrations and history lessons on hand-spinning, weaving, and dyeing yarn. Participants listen to bagpipes and the delicate sounds of the harp. Children will be thrilled and amazed while watching jugglers, minstrels, acrobats, jousting knights, and dancing around the traditional maypole with village maidens and fairies. Other activities include human chess games and a child's parade of knights, jesters, and minstrels.

Tracing Your Family Tree—Offer a workshop taught by local genealogist to provide the skills necessary to trace the family's history. Participants learn what public and private records are available and how to gain access to them. Techniques for recordkeeping and interpretation of old records will be discussed.

Destination Downtown

Downtown events planned as family entertainment options have become one of the fastest growing types of events. Municipal planners and downtown merchants recognize events as a significant way to drive people to their establishments.

Antiques on the Road—Everyone is talking about what they have in their attic that may or may not be an antique. This is an opportunity for people to bring their antiques and have them appraised by the local antique stores experts. The charge of $5 per item helps to offset event expenses. A great addition is a quick class and demonstration on how to get started in collecting antiques, what to look for in an antique, which items bring the highest price, appreciation and depreciation of investments, antique construction techniques, and how to determine if a piece is a fake. As an added element, invite a local antique collector to sponsor a show-and-tell display.

Catch a Deal on Main Street—Hold a flea market for fishing, camping, boating, and hunting enthusiasts. Individuals' pay $15 fee for a 10-foot by 10-foot space to sell or trade their outdoor equipment. Charge commercial vendors $100 to set up shop in a 20-foot by 20-foot space. Great deals are offered as well as entertainment such as bluegrass music and demonstrations. For children, offer rod-and-reel casting contests that test their skills and earn prizes.

Clownin' Around Downtown—Everyone comes to clown around downtown and watch real clowns in action, while learning magic tricks and how to do balloon sculpting.

Community Garage Sale—Turn the community center into a giant garage sale. Participants rent a 12-foot by 12-foot space which includes one 6-foot table and one chair. Bargain hunters come to shop no matter what the weather.

Cool Cars Under the Stars—Hold an antique, classic, and collectible car show once a week during the summer in a downtown parking lot or on Main Street. Adopt a different theme for each week, such as street rod, Olds, sports car, muscle car, import, vintage motorcycle, Cadillac, and Corvette nights. Provide live entertainment and invite downtown restaurants to set up a food booth outside of their business.

Downtown Rock Hunting—Plan a rock hunt downtown to get participants familiar with the downtown area as well as the local architecture. An amazing assortment of rocks, minerals, and fossils can be found in the various buildings and structures.

Downtown Showcase: Savor the Flavor, Savor the Fun—This is an event sponsored by the municipality, chamber of commerce, convention and visitors bureau, and the downtown business association. Invite employees in a position of recommending restaurants or facilitating groups to your downtown, and show them all there is to offer. A packet of information containing copies of downtown restaurant menus, retail store information, and maps of historic buildings should be compiled to give to each attendee. Each business donates door prizes to be given away to participants. Each restaurant donates one plate of hors d'oeuvres for the function.

Get Downtown and Dirty—This is a great promotion for Earth Day (April 22), with local organizations, civic groups, and individual volunteers joining in a clean-up effort in an area (downtown, park, or river) that needs help in picking up debris and litter, removing graffiti, and planting flowers.

Stair Climb—The Cystic Fibrosis Foundation Stair Climb is more than just an alternative to a 10K run. Participants race in your community's tallest building. The Stair Climb is an event that celebrates pride, spirit, and the willingness to go the distance to help others. Those who climb all the way to the top, either individually or as part of a three-person team, will have triumphed over a man-made challenge. It will be tough, but fun. Are participants up to the challenge? Individual competition includes separate men and women's divisions. Team competition has teams consisting of three members, with each covering one third of the distance and passing the baton in relay fashion. Top award is a "stair master." After the climb, participants and spectators gather at a "Survivors' Party" giving everyone a chance to meet and mingle with the other people who climbed as well as those who cheered.

Summertime Sizzling Sidewalk Sale—Kick off the spring or summer season with an annual sidewalk sale to promote downtown businesses, boost retail sales, and create excitement for other downtown activities. Merchants bring out sale items and display them on sidewalks. One can promote the event by offering free parking in municipal garages when a merchant signs a voucher.

Ultimate Scavenger Hunt—If you can read and solve riddles, this is the challenge for you. Participants learn about the characteristics of the local community by figuring out the answers that will lead you to the next clue. Teams travel in automobiles going from one clue site to another. The hunt takes place at night, and flashlights are necessary. Participants bring their maps, odds and ends, and their thinking caps. Clues include word puzzles, pictorial anagrams, complicated map readings, and telephone book entries. Each challenge is to find where the next clue is hidden. A team can consist of as many people as can fit into an automobile. An assortment of prizes is awarded. Examples of clues include

- How many times does the word garlic appear on ___________ restaurant's menu?
- What is the name of the local theater (give theater name) current play?
- How many tennis courts are at ________ park?
- Find a bar of soap from the ________ hotel.
- What is the date on the gravestone next to the _________ in the local cemetery?

Valentine Surprise—This is a wonderful way to promote the local businesses. Create a brochure listing cooperating restaurants, spas, florists, hotels, and gift stores. Participants answer questions related to Valentine's Day and the local businesses. Winners are selected and receive special Valentine's Day gifts donated by the businesses, including boxes of chocolates, flowers, spa visits, and a grand prize package offering accommodations for two at a local hotel.

Everyone Loves a Parade

Armed Forces Day Parade—The purpose of this parade is to honor and recognize active, retired, and deceased men and women of the U.S. Armed Forces for their service to the nation. Appropriately decorated vehicles will be admitted as entries, including military vehicles with approval from a parade committee.

International Parade—Kick off this weekend festival with a parade featuring the different countries represented in the community. Entries may include German dancers, Irish and Scottish Bagpipes, Mexican and Chinese Dragons, and West African Folk Dancers.

Music Man Parade—Music is in the air! All trombones are invited to march down Main Street to open a special event. Popular songs from the Gay Nineties are played.

Parade of Boats—Spectators will be delighted with the procession of lighted vessels as they travel down your local river, lake front, or harbor. The evening ends with a spectacular fireworks display.

Fiesta!

American Graffiti—A giant wall mural of previously drawn images is a great hands-on community project for festival guests. As in the traditional paint-by-numbers books, participants fill in the blanks with paint.

Bachelor Auction—This is a great fundraiser for your local nonprofit. One should solicit the communities' most eligible bachelors, as well as local restaurants, spas, and date packages. The men and date packages are then auctioned off to the highest bidder.

Bartender's Mix-Off/Bartender's Best—A chance for bartenders to put their talent where their mouths are with an exciting show of talent, skill, and speed. The communities' top bartenders compete in competitions such as smoothest piña colada and ultimate martini. Cash prizes and awards are presented. See Appendix 10.1 (p. 85) for an example of Bartender's Mix-Off rules and procedures.

Basketball Slam Dunk Competition—A lowered outdoor basketball hoop is used and teens compete for creative dunks. Teens will compete in two rounds with three dunks per person in each round. Prizes awarded to the top three finishers.

Beer Festival—Everyone is invited downtown for a day of microbrew tasting. Feature American and international ales, lagers, stouts, specialty brews, and pilsners, while offering information on home brewing and a beer tasting contest. Have lots of live entertainment and plenty of food. Festival guests pay $25, which includes unlimited two-ounce beer samples and a complimentary beer festival collector's mug.

Beer Tasting Competition—This offers fun competition for the malt, wheat, and hops connoisseur. Participants who guess eight beers correctly will win a prize. Sample size is two ounces.

Booths With a Cause—This is a special area at the event for nonprofit organizations to promote their causes and solicit donations. Political groups, churches, social activists, and charities make their pitches to passing festival-goers. *Note*: Have a specific policy regarding do's and don'ts for this area which may include selling products, size and the number of signs and posters, and so forth.

Castle of Can Food—This is a great way for your Taste of the Town Festival to support the local food bank. With the help of a radio sponsor, ask festival attendees to bring canned food to build a large castle during the event. At the end of festival, all canned food is donated to food charity.

Celebrity Baby Photo Contest—Participants match the photos to the names of local celebrities. All correct answers will be entered into a drawing for a festival prize package.

Children's Court/Kids Rule!—Designate an area within the festival specifically for children. Participants have the opportunity to enjoy a wide variety of activities, games, storytellers, arts and crafts, music, dance, and sing-alongs. Additional program ideas include face painting, punk hair styles, MASH tent (fake finger cast, fake wounds), Lego exhibits, local mascots, sidewalk chalk drawing contest, puppet shows, diaper changing area, and an International Children's Area (e.g., piñata, international songs and games, international paper art).

Chili Cook-Off—Invite anyone with that "famous" chili recipe to enter and compete for cash and prizes. Contestants can enter in either professional or novice categories, as well as compete for a people's choice award. For only $5.00, guests can taste samples of the best chili in the area, from seasoned professionals to grandma's secret recipe. Appendices 10.2 (p. 86), 10.3 (p. 90), and 10.4 (p. 91) includes examples for Chili Cook-Off rules and regulations, registration forms, and judging sheets.

Chocolate Festival—This festival features treats ranging from torte and cheesecake to fudge and dipped fruits. Professional chefs compete in chocolate sculpting and demonstrations making edible baskets, leaves, and other garnishes. For $5.00, the spectator is entitled to ten tastes of chocolate items.

Coffee Connoisseurs—Everyone enjoys the finer tastes in life as they learn brewing techniques, information on all types of java, and the best places in town to find the perfect beans. Sample tastes for everyone. This activity is a great alternative to beer tasting or wine tasting.

Cooking School/Look Who's Cooking—Distinguished chefs from the local area demonstrate their tricks of the trade at the local festival. Spectators learn master food preparation and cooking techniques as well as secrets to some favorite dishes from local chefs.

Daily News Letter—This is a great way to let vendors or artist know what is going on during the festival. Tidbits of information (weather reports, crowd estimates) are collected and printed overnight. It is helpful to obtain a sponsor to name the Daily News.

Double Dare Challenge—Designed after the fear-based reality TV shows, this challenge pits contestants against each other and their own fears.

Feeling Sporty—One may offer numerous sports competitions throughout your festival weekend. Participants compete for prizes while participating in activities such as half court shot, slam dunk competition, three-point shooting competition, home run derby, three-on-three basketball shootout, and the like.

Festival Scavenger Hunt—Give participants clues to different festival components. They must answer a series of questions with a drawing from all correct winners for prizes.

Get Your Act Together—No real talent required, just the desire to try your hand at entertaining the crowd. Try a musical instrument (provided), sing, dance, perform a comedy routine, or just clown around. Festival coupons and prizes awarded to all that participate.

Grocery Store Sampling Pavilion—Under one large tent, a local grocery store invites their food vendors to offer samples of their products.

Husband Calling Contest—In this hilarious contest wives yell for their husbands and the audience chooses the winner.

Ice Carving Competition—Ice carvers use their skills and chainsaws to create unique and beautiful masterpieces out of solid blocks of ice. Spectators listen to the roar of the chainsaws and watch the ice fly. Appendix 10.5 (p. 92) has an example of ice carving contest rules and regulations.

Jalapeño Pepper Eating Contest—Running nose? Watery Eyes? Begging for Water? It must be the Jalapeño Pepper Eating Contest! This contest will have spectators and participants screaming and crying with agony and joy. Each participant is given 20 jalapeños and one minute. The first contestant to eat the 20 peppers under the time limit wins. Should the time limit expire, the contestant who has devoured the most peppers will be declared the "winner." Contestants must be 21 years of age to enter. Cash prizes are awarded. Appendix 10.6 (p. 93) has an example of jalapeño pepper eating contest rules and regulations.

Jigsaw Challenge—This is a fun race to completion with 500-piece jigsaw puzzles in three divisions: 14 and under, 15 and up, and seniors (55 or older). Charge $5.00 per team (maximum of four members per team).

Jubilee Jam—This festival provides entertainment ranging from melodramatic to whimsical. There will be magic shows, modern dance and ballet, ethnic performances, and costumed dancers. Food vendors will tempt festival-goers with delectable treats in the food court.

Kids Kingdom/Kids Korner/Kids Corral—This is a special place at the festival with activities and entertainment just for children. A facade or entryway that children will recognize and beg their parents to enter should be built to include sidewalk chalk art, bubbles, and lots of hands-on art projects (e.g., Creation Station). Enlist a local group of college students to build a chicken wire structure in the kids' kingdom for children to help decorate throughout the weekend. One should solicit the local paint store to donate open cans of paints for art activities such as giant wall mural, paint a bus, or help Michelangelo paint the Sistine chapel (children must lay down on the ground and paint a pre-drawn picture), paint a smile on Mona Lisa (4-foot by 8-foot wooden panels with black-and-white photo of the Mona Lisa with her smile blanked out).

Lost and Found—Place an antique fire truck near the children's area to serve as the lost-and-found station for the event. Parents tell children, "if you get lost go to the fire truck," where there are plenty of volunteers to provide juice and cookies while the parents are being sought.

Nose Pickin'—Have couples try to pick their partner's nose. Have several men sit in a row, cover them with a large sheet with small holes cut so each man can stick his nose through the hole. The female tries to pick which nose belongs to her partner.

Paul Bunyan Festival—A family event featuring log rolling, tree chopping, ax throwing, tree climbing, and log splitting contests.

Poetry Board—The perfect addition to the arts festival or reading festival. Provide a large metal poetry wall with magnetic words for participants to arrange and rearrange as they choose—a large version of the refrigerator game. If your festival falls on a holiday, have special theme words with the appropriate holiday color (e.g., for St. Patrick's Day festival, "green" words, Irish, clover).

Poetry Sandwich—Local and regional poetry performers present "bite-size" poetry "sandwiches" between musical entertainment acts.

Poetry Slam—Got the groove for spoken word? Poetry slams pit poet against poet. Express your creativity, spirituality, and emotions through poetry. A panel of judges, selected from the audience scores competing poets on a scale of 1–10. Guidelines for the slammers: all poetry must be original work, performed in under three minutes, and no props are allowed. Offer cash prizes for winners.

Puppets on Parade—A promenade of puppets strolling through your festival accompanied by live music. Festival committee members create puppets of larger-than-life creatures, such as ladybugs, butterflies, fish, and trees. Make puppets from foam, fabric, and colored paper.

Restaurant Pentathlon—At your *Taste of the Town* festival, offer a trophy and cash prize to the most decorated restaurant in the festival. Restaurants compete in five disciplines: Waiter's Race, Silver Spoon Competition, Tent Decoration, Bartender's Mix-Off, and Chili Cook-Off. Appendix 10.7 (p. 94) has an example of pentathlon rules and regulations.

Rod and Custom Show/Show and Shine—A display of classics, hot rods, and vintage vehicles. Judge vehicles in the following categories: antique, classic, street rod, custom, street machine, super street, and best of show. Add an auto parts flea market with a $15 charge for each 12-foot space.

Salsa Sunday—Host a community dance party at your next festival for those who love to dance.

Sand Sculpture—Build sand sculpture pits using hay bales and fine coarse sand. Have a water hose with a nozzle nearby so competitors can keep their sand moist during the competitions. Invite local architectural firms to challenge each other for the architect's award. Challenge festival-goers to create the best design in two different categories: ages 5 to 11 and ages 12 and up. Solicit local sand and concrete companies, or brick and mortar companies to sponsor the area.

Sidewalk Chalk—Block off a section of the street within the festival for children and adults to draw their interpretation of this year's festival theme to create a colorful patchwork of chalk art.

Skills and Thrills/Teen Zone/Teen Extreme/Raise the Roof—Teenagers will love a challenging area within your festival that includes rock climbing, an iron man obstacle course, jousting, a climbing wall, a giant Twister contest, radar pitch (throwing baseballs at a target with a radar gun displaying ball speed), micro race cars, a bungee run, and the U.S. Marine Corps Chin-Up Challenge. Include an area where they can make their own video (dress in costume, pick out their own song, and get a copy of the video to take home).

Spirit Garden—Include an area within your festival where alcohol may be served and consumed.

Spring Break Dance—Teens join their friends on Main Street for a spring break dance with music provided by local live bands. Businesses sponsor the dance and have a booth on the site to promote their services and products to teens (e.g., cell phone companies, music stores, clothing stores).

Spring Fling—Food, beverages, and live music make for an enjoyable spring weekend.

Stage Right Party—A sponsor can purchase this space, and leave the party up to the festival planners. Provide catering, tables, chairs, beverages, decorations, and other supplies. The purchasing sponsor invites only their guests to enjoy the area right beside the main stage. You can also sell this space to bus groups for use when they come to the event.

Street Theater—Create full-size street figures out of wood or heavy cardboard and place them around town prior to the festival to draw attention to the upcoming event. Place the "people" near crosswalks, sitting on benches, and walking their dogs. This is a guarantee to draw lots of pre-event media attention. To take an event from ordinary to festive, add street theaters throughout the festival. Be creative with placement so festival-goers seek out these performances. Examples include jugglers, guitarist, comedians, fire-eaters, artists, mimes, stilt walkers, and costume characters.

Swinging' Under the Moonlight—The music of the big band era will get the participants' feet stomping and heads bobbing. Everyone jumps and jives to an old sound that is the hottest in town. For those whose jitterbug skills are a little rusty, offer free swing lessons and basic steps, kicks, timing, and turns. Everyone comes dressed to impress because great prizes will be awarded.

Taste of the Town—Invite local restaurants to participate by offering the public a taste of their culinary specialties. A food festival can help local restaurants to promote their businesses and menus by engaging with customers outside of their standard patronage. Set a maximum price that restaurants can charge for each item for consumers to sample a variety of taste items. Limit restaurant menu items to not duplicate specific dishes. Encourage restaurants to decorate their booths to make the event more pleasing to the attendees. Festival-goers may cast votes for *Peoples Choice Award* for the restaurant serving their favorite food (see Appendix 10.8 [p. 95] for a People's Choice Award ballot). Incorporate a cooking school or culinary corner where local chefs will demonstrate their talents. Add a wine tasting area, ice carving competition where chefs work their magic with blocks of ice, a waiters' race, and a bartenders' mix-off (see *Restaurant Pentathlon*).

Taste of the Town Cookbook—Competing restaurants submit their favorite recipes to be complied in a *Taste of the Town* cookbook, with proceeds benefiting a local food bank. A fun spinoff is to get participating restaurants to provide homemade or "secret" recipes for the cookbook. Compile the recipes with each missing one essential ingredient. The only way to get the missing ingredient is by visiting the restaurant after the event.

Tent Decorating Contest—Pit food vendors against each other for the best decorated tent. Offer cash prizes to vendors taking the most pride in their appearance. Creativity and imagination are key.

Touch a Truck—Kids love big trucks. A festival display of various trucks and vehicles for kids to get a closer look and touch. Examples include ambulance, police car, race car, fire truck, school bus, antique limousine, police motorcycle, dump truck, caterpillar, Coast Guard boat, and Army tank.

Video Dance Party—Offer for teenagers only from 9:00 p.m.–11:00 p.m. with their own area at the event.

Waiters' Race— Spectators watch the "best of the best" waiters compete against each other, as well as the official time clock. The servers must demonstrate skill, balance, and dexterity as they race through an obstacle course with a full tray.

Wine Festival—Participants will learn how to taste wine and explore wine varieties in a festive setting. Everyone has the opportunity to sample the selection of wines while savoring gourmet dishes and enjoying live entertainment. Participants also will learn about aroma and taste characteristics, how wines are made, how to read wine labels, how to find wine values, and how to prepare food to match the wine selection. Add a silent art auction so that participants can purchase their favorite wine by the bottle or case. Everyone takes home a collector's wine glass, engraved with the event logo and presenting sponsor.

Kids' Korner

Children are optimists willing to experiment and learn. They love new ideas and are into technology. Offer plenty of creative interaction, while understanding that they have their own way of viewing the world.

ArtWise Day Camp/Art of Nature/The Nature of Art—The goal of this coed, week-long day camp for children ages 8 to 12 is to help children to develop various skills, such as concentration, planning, creative problem solving, awareness, observation, and imagination as they work with the fun-loving subject of nature. A local artist instructs the camp, children spend time both inside and outside, drawing, playing, building, observing, and completing awareness exercises. Represent the art of nature by having the children draw objects from life, experiment with different textures and a variety of mediums, and become aware of the cycles of life in nature and the connection among all natural things. While representing the nature of art through concentration on elements of design, shape, and color, encourage spontaneous expression and individual creative energy expressed through artwork. A guest speaker is the highlight of one day, and a trip to the zoo to observe and draw the animals is another.

Community Dance Company—The goal of the dance company is to reduce antisocial behavior through the discipline of dance and to promote health and nutrition as the preferred way of life. The dance company invites young ladies, grades 4–8, to meet three nights per week for two hours each day for dance instruction (including traditional

African dance as well as Contemporary American dance) with an additional 30 minutes devoted to academic studies. In addition to dance, the company teaches etiquette, public speaking, and other esteem-building activities.

The dance company operates under strict regulations that demand academic success as a prerequisite to participate in the program. The goal is to reduce school absenteeism, improve academic skills, improve social skills, improve personal attitudes, increase exposure to cultural experiences, and increase community pride and unity.

Community Gardening Program—Children learn to grow flowers and vegetables and then get to reap the fruits of their labor.

Kids Flea Market—"One person's junk is another person's treasure," so participants can make money while getting rid of items that they no longer use. This event teaches children the basics of entrepreneurship. For a basic fee ($5.00), children ages 8 to 15 rent a 10-foot space with a table. Guidelines include the following: All items must be less than $10.00 each, all items must be child-oriented, and no food or beverages. Suggested items for sale include board games, trading cards, video games, action figures, and sports equipment.

Kids on Course: Getting Kids off the Streets and on the Fairways—A program for youth ages 8 to 15 in which they are taught the fundamentals of golf. This six-week program focuses not only on golf lessons, but also on the etiquette and rules of the game. Because golf requires a lot of self-discipline, the participants gain self-respect, respect for others, and respect for others' property. As the participants learn the game, they build self-esteem and self-confidence. *Kids On Course* promotes success through skills training and practice, healthy competition, camaraderie with others, and teamwork.

Once a week the children meet with a golf pro at a local golf center to receive lessons. At the end of the six-week program, the goal is for the participants to be able to complete a Par 3 course while adhering to the rules of the game. After completing the lessons, each participant is provided with free passes to a golf center to play free rounds of golf. One should ask for equipment to be donated by local sporting goods store for the participants to check out for practice.

Kids' Koncerts—A series of clowns, mimes, musicians, and magicians perform on a stage for children audiences.

Kids' Pets on Parade—Children bring their favorite pet to show off. Organizers should create awards for most well-behaved, best trick, and best of show.

Kids' Day—A day designed to celebrate children and encourage adults to spend time with them. Include Boys and Girls Clubs of America, 4-H clubs, YMCA, YWCA, Girl Scouts, and Boy Scouts. (National Kids Day activity guide and other information available at www.kidsday.net.)

Latch-Key Survival Skills—Design this program to help children to cope when moms and dads are not home. Topics include cooking, home safety, kitchen safety, and following directions.

Luau Splash Party—Kids participate in limbo contests, eat watermelon, and try their hand at pineapple art—attaching colorful pieces of paper, small drink umbrellas, flowers and so forth to their very own pineapple.

Recyclable Art—Children learn fun things that they can do to make their world a better place to live. Kids use recyclable materials to create arts and crafts projects.

Rent-A-Teen Workshop—Teens 14 to 17 register for this program and are taught interviewing skills, how to complete job applications, and basic work skills for jobs, such as childcare and yard work.

Rodeo Keg Riding—This great aquatic activity adds fun to any pool party. Put an empty beverage keg in the deep end of the pool, the participants swim out to it, try to mount it, and then once on, ride it for as long as possible. Have a couple people in the water to keep the keg away from the edges.

Teen Talent Transformation—Middle and high school teens compete for the best talent sponsored by a local radio station who provides the karaoke machine for the background music and words to the songs. Teens can sing a solo, in a duo, or in a group. Give promotional CD for best performance.

Xtreme Teens—This program allows teens to experience activities such as white-water rafting, rock climbing, ice skating, canoeing, kayaking, fishing, camping, and hiking.

Learning Made Fun

Celebrate Reading Festival/Downtown Book Festival/ Reading on the River—Create a reading festival to focus the community's attention on the importance and enjoyment of reading. Contact the local newspaper for support in promoting the event, inviting local authors to participate, and donating newsprint for art projects. The children's activity area includes arts and crafts activities, parade of story book characters, and "Bodacious Books," where children learn to create and bind their own books. The local library, nonprofit literacy organizations, Rotary Club, or United Way can offer book give-a-ways, book swaps, and tips on parenting and literacy.

The *Celebrate Reading Festival* provides the community with a fun-filled event focused on literacy. Besides being entertained by the poets, musicians, storytellers, celebrity readers and authors, those in attendance learn of local agencies dedicated to literacy and education. Children and parents are taught the importance of reading and are encouraged to read together. Adults are given the opportunity to join various volunteer groups.

This day-long festival is preceded by a week of literary events, including lectures, panel discussions, and storytelling at various schools and libraries. During the week, several book retailers promote the festival by offering special discounts and for hosting book signing by *Celebrate Reading* featured authors. On the day of the festival, these book retailers, including local college bookstores, have a book display of new and used books for sale. The festival includes four stages of continuous entertainment: authors, children's, songwriters/poetry, and drama. A unique promotional tip: Produce bookmarks with the event logo, dates, and times to distribute for free prior to the event at local libraries, bookstores, and coffee shops.

Tall Tales/Tell It in the Mountains—This storytelling festival highlights novice and professional storytellers. Come watch as characters are brought to life with the narrative skills of the masterful tale spinners.

Tell Me a Story Contest—The contest promotes the art of storytelling, and develops self-confidence and public speaking skills. Participants compete by grade levels and tell any variety of stories, such as folk tales, fables, fairy tales, or legends (no poems). The student must "tell" the story from a published work but word-for-word memorization is not required. The story time limit is 10 minutes, the use of gestures is optional, and notes are not allowed. Judging is based on enunciation and pronunciation, eye contact, poise, volume and voice inflection, and how well the story is told.

Win a Rose for Mom —Participants submit an essay using 200 words or less, explaining why their Mom is the "World's Greatest Mom." Essays are judged on style, content, and creativity. The essays must be personal, original works. This essay contest—with categories for children ages 8 to 12 years—challenges children to examine and define why their Moms are important to them. Moms of the winning entry in each category will be delivered a red rose and the wining essay on Mother's Day.

Writers' Workshop—Release the writer inside you! Each year, offer an original writer's workshop by exploring the four basics of all fiction: setting, character, plot, and theme. Get local bookstores or writing groups to cosponsor the workshop by providing budding authors a chance to learn from and interact with some of the nation's best writers and novelists. A three-day workshop may include writing exercises, a question-and-answer session, lectures, public readings, and book signings by the guest authors. A highlight of the workshop can be a personal conference with a guest author, where he or she critiques one work by each of the participants and provides individual suggestions and comments.

Music Series and Concerts

Parks, downtown plazas, amphitheaters, or even a block of Main Street are excellent locations for a spring and summer concert series. Communities love free outdoor concerts, plays, and performances. A concert series can become one of the most popular components on a community event calendar. Concerts vary by location, size, type of music, day of the week, and whether there is an admission charge. Concerts can be great assets for downtown by spotlighting the area and keeping or bringing people to the area.

Bag Day Lunch/Lunchtime on the Lawn—What better way to spend a lunch hour than out in the spring or fall sun, listening to an assortment of entertainment? Set up a series of concerts in a park or outside plaza area that is convenient for workers to eat their lunch and enjoy free entertainment. Print the schedule of performances on a brown paper bag or on a flyer inviting the public to lunch.

Pickin' in the Park—Delight in an old fashioned "pickin' and grinning" jam session, and invite everyone to participate. Bring your fiddle, banjo, or guitar.

Summer Concert Series—During the months of June, July, and August from 7:00 p.m.–9:00 p.m. offer a series of concerts at the local outdoor theater or in a community park. Invite area residents to bring their picnic blankets and dinner to enjoy the free entertainment. Select a different style of music each week. Don't forget to book a patriotic group for the 4th of July week. Name a concert series to fit the setting, such as

- *A Garden Affaire*
- *A Summer's Night Music Series*
- *Concerts in the Garden*
- *Downtown Alive/Alive Downtown*
- *Downtown After Five/Alive After Five*
- *Folktown*—Music presented in a coffeehouse atmosphere
- *Hot City Nights/Hot Summer Nights*—A nighttime summer series in the middle of downtown
- *Jammin' July*
- *Main Street Jazz/Downtown Jazz*—Free Friday evening entertainment on Main Street USA. Offer a variety of food and beverages with a mix of jazz and blues bands.
- *Out to Lunch*—A noonday concert series offering downtown workers and visitors music of every genre, including folk, jazz, pop, country, and swing
- *Pops in the Park*
- *River Nighttime Series*

- *Reggae Nights/Reggae on the River*—The sounds and rhythms of reggae music will have participants moving to an island beat.
- *Rhythms of the Region/Rhythm on the River*
- *Saturday Night Live*
- *Summer Breeze Jazz*—An evening of smooth jazz presented in your local amphitheater or main street plaza.
- *Summer Stage*
- *Summer Twilight Series*
- *"TGIF"*—Start the weekend off with an evening filled with great music and the perfect opportunity to see and been seen

Tiny Tots

Art in the Park—A creative experience for children with an emphasis on making art with items they can find in the park.

Artistic Birthday Parties—Offer birthday parties at the local community/recreation center with art projects included. Tie-dye T-shirts, decorate tennis shoes, make clay works, make paper projects, and decorate masks.

Gigglin' Gourmets/Kids Are Cookin'—Teach 3- to 5-year-olds kitchen safety skills, table manners, and good nutrition. There will be fun in the cookin' and in the eating.

Happy Hour—Plan an action-packed hour to play with hoops, balls, and music.

Itsy Bitsy Art—A creative workshop designed to teach 3- to 5-year-olds the fun in creating their own masterpiece.

Kids Rock—Kids have fun while learning to develop balance, motor skills, and listening skills. Participants exercise and move with the music, such as the Chicken Dance, the Hokey Pokey, and the Twist.

Little Anglers—Youngsters get a taste of fishing by rotating through eight learning stations that cover topics of casting, knots, fish habitat, safety skills, and conservation talks. The event planner provides the equipment and lets the children try their new skills and fish.

Mad Hatters' Tea Party—Children dress up in their finest apparel to join the tea party with games, refreshments, and prizes. Planners should tell participants "do not forget to wear a hat!"

Music, Mommy, and Me—Singing, rhythm, movement, listening skills, and finger preparation for keyboard are explored together by teacher, parent, and child.

Storytelling for Youngsters—This can be as simple as having someone read two or three short stories a day.

Teddy Bear Tea—Participants bring their teddy bears with the option to enter him or her in a contest for largest, smallest, best dressed, most unique, best loved, and best of show. While enjoying tea and cookies, children listen to stories featuring bears.

Appendix 10.1: Bartenders' Mix-Off Rules and Procedures

1. There will be a total of 3 rounds
   - Round 1: Bartender against bartender in a head-to-head elimination. The winner advances to Round 2.
   - Round 2: Bartender against the clock. The two best times will advance to Round 3.
   - Round 3: Bartenders with the top two times against each other for the title of *Master Mixer*. 3rd, 4th, and 5th places will be determined by the remaining fastest times in Round 2.

2. The Master of Ceremonies (MC) chooses a card at random from the tip jar. The card lists the names of three mixed drinks, one beer, and one wine. The MC will read the orders out loud and on his or her direction, the contestants will begin mixing drinks. Bartenders will have the option of using a pencil and pad to make notes of the orders. Participants will be required to begin with hands behind their backs. When a contestant has completed the ordered drinks, he or she will ring the bell provided. A panel of at least two judges will preside over the competition. The bartender with the best time will advance.

3. Penalty Points
   - 10-second penalty per drink if not placed on cocktail napkin.
   - 15-second penalty if wine is less than four ounces or more than six ounces.
   - 15-second penalty if mixed drink does not contain proper garnish.
   - 15-second penalty for improper layering of drink.
   - 30-second penalty for any drink knocked over (broken glass penalty will also apply if applicable).
   - 30-second penalty per drink if cocktail is made with the wrong ingredients.
   - 30-second penalty per drink made in wrong glass.
   - 30-second penalty for wrong beer or wine.
   - 60-second penalty for each broken glass.
   - 90-second penalty for each omitted drink.

4. Liter bottles will be used for all mixed drinks. In Rounds 1 and 2, wine bottles will be uncorked. In Round 3, contestants will be required to open bottles. Beer will not be opened or poured, but must be placed on a napkin. All five drinks must be placed on top of the bar.

5. If a bartender misses his or her call, he or she will automatically be disqualified and his or her opponent will race for practice in Round 1 and for time in Round 2.

6. ***Sportsmanship Rule***: Any contestant may be ejected for unsportsmanlike behavior as deemed necessary by the contest supervisor.

7. All rulings by the judges are final.

Appendix 10.2: Annual Chili Cook-Off Rules and Regulations

General Information

Location: Main Street in Downtown *Anytown, USA*

Admission: $5.00 for tasting ticket. Cook-off open to general public.

Registration

Applications must be received by deadline date. *Late applications received between* Date *and* Date *will be charged a $25 late registration fee. Applications will not be accepted after* Date. *No Exceptions!* Please send applications to:

Festival Name
Attn: *Committee Chair Name*
P.O. Box 1234
Anytown, USA 12345
(123) 555–6789, Fax: (123) 555–1234
E-mail: eventname@website.com

Chili Teams

Chili teams can consist of up to four people. The entry fee is $50 for the Professional Category and $35.00 for the Novice Category. Any team or individual who has participated in the Chili Cook-Off for more than three years will be considered "Professional." In addition, any chef or food-related employee of a full-service restaurant will be considered "Professional." Each team will receive up to four official Chili Cook-Off T-shirts, 1,000 one-ounce sample cups, one 14-foot by 14-foot exhibitor space, and four tickets to the event.

Booth Display

You may set up your booth on *Friday, Date*, beginning at 9:00 a.m. Selection of booth location will be on a first-come basis. All Chili Teams are responsible for bringing their own tents. To participate, health department requires all teams to have a tent for "coverage purposes." Booths have no running water or electricity. Water will be made available at a designated area. A sample packing list to bring to the cook-off could include

- Cooking stove, propane, Coleman fuel, or other heating element
- Fire extinguisher
- Coolers with ice for food
- Cooking pots
- Tables/chairs
- Backdrop
- Utensils
- Sample spoons

Rules and Regulations

1. Chili cannot be precooked or prepared prior to competition. Start time is 1:00 p.m. Ingredients may be prechopped prior to start time. Precooked meat (before 1:00 p.m.) will disqualify your team's chili. Exceptions include vegetables, sauces, and spice mixes.
2. Professionals must cook a 10-gallon minimum of chili and novice must cook a 5-gallon minimum. One quart of chili from each team needs to be reserved for judging.
3. Please be aware of your Team's liability for the wholesomeness and safety of your chili as it will be consumed. All competitors are subject to inspection by health department. NO ANIMALS will be permitted into the event area.
4. Competitors must furnish their own cooking utensils and heat source. NO OPEN FIRES!!
5. All entries must be ready for judging by 7:00 p.m. The lead cook will present the judging sample. Winners and prizes will be awarded from event headquarters at 9:30 p.m.
6. Your entry fee entitles you to one 14-foot by 14-foot exhibition space. Tents or coverings are supplied by the Applicant/Participant. These must be 14-foot by 14-foot or smaller.
7. Teams are NOT ALLOWED to sell any food or novelties to the public during this event. Sampling should be limited to the one-ounce cups provided.
8. NO ALCOHOLIC BEVERAGES are to be distributed or sold to the public. In addition, consumption of alcoholic beverages/open containers on festival site before 5:00 p.m. *Friday, Date* is prohibited.

9. A mandatory Head Cooks meeting will be held at 12:00 noon to review contest rules. One member from each Team must be present.
10. Contest will be held rain or shine.
11. ***Sportsmanship rule***: Any Team or Team Member may be ejected for unsportsmanlike behavior as deemed by the contest supervisor.

Judging

- The Annual Chili Cook-Off judges will sample and score all entries. Their decisions are final.
- Each entry will be judged on three criteria and scored 1 to 10 (10 being the highest). The three criteria are: Team Spirit, Appearance, and Taste (x 2). (Taste scores will be weighted double.)
- Each entry will be judged on its own merit and will not be compared with any other. The scores from the judges will determine the winners. Remember, just because it's hot, doesn't make it good.

Prizes: Best Chili Awards

	Professional	Novice
First Place	$1,000	$500
Second Place	$400	$250
Third Place	$200	$100

People's Choice and Overall Best: $150

Time Table

9:00 a.m.	Set-Up
12:00 p.m.	Head Cook Meeting (Review of Rules)
1:00 p.m.	Cooking Begins
5:00 p.m.	*Event Name* Opens
5:00 p.m.	Judging Begins
6:00 p.m.	Awards
8:30 p.m.	People's Choice Award

Terms of Participation

1. Promotion: *Event Name* shall list the Chili Cook-Off teams in the event program.
2. The participating Restaurant/Team shall provide adequate personnel for serving chili.
3. The availability of business cards, matches, menus, and other advertising by the participating Restaurants/Teams is encouraged but not required.
4. The participating Restaurant/Team shall comply with rules and regulations of the *Anytown, USA* and the *State of Anystate* and participating Restaurant/Team agrees to hold harmless *Event Name*, its officers, directors, representatives, employees, and agents from any penalties, fines, costs, expenses or damages from the participating Restaurant's/Team's failure to do so.
5. The participating Restaurant/Team shall provide *Event Name* with a copy of its business insurance policy, indicating liability coverage.
6. The participating Restaurant/Team shall be maintained in a neat, safe and orderly condition. The participating Restaurant/Team shall remove all rubbish and trash on a regular basis to a trash receptacle.
7. The participating Restaurant/Team shall insure that all cooking elements are in a good state of repair. All cooking elements will be subject to inspection by the *Town of Anytown, USA* and any hazardous elements may be required to be eliminated or relocated to insure safety.
8. The participating Restaurant/Team shall be responsible for setting up and removing its own equipment, fixtures, decorations and other property.
9. *Event Name* shall be responsible for cleaning up used serving items and other trash in the common area during the event.
10. Liability: Neither *Event Name, Anytown, USA,* nor any adjacent property owner shall be liable for any loss or damage to the property of the participating Restaurant/Team, or of its representatives, employees, agents, patrons, and guests because of fire, robbery, accidents, or any other cause whatsoever that may arise from the

participating Restaurant's/Team's use or occupancy of its tasting center(s). The participating Restaurant/Team agrees to indemnify and hold harmless *Event Name* and its officers, directors, representatives, employees and agents, and the *Anytown, USA*, its employees and agents, against any and all claims of any person whomsoever, arising from the acts or omission of the participating Restaurants/Teams, its representatives, employees, agents, patrons or guests.

11. Failure to Hold Chili Cook-Off: In the event that *Event Name* is not held for any reason whatsoever, the participating Restaurant/Team shall be entitled to a refund of the fee it paid to reserve its space and the participating Restaurant/Team hereby releases *Event Name*, and its respective officers, directors, representatives, employees, and agents from any and all claims for damages that may arise in consequence of *Event Name* not being held.
12. Termination: *Event Name* may, at its election, terminate the Participation Agreement between *Event Name* and the participating Restaurant/Team at any time on the breach of the participating Restaurant/Team of any of the terms, provisions and conditions set forth in the said Participation Agreement and upon and after such termination, the participating Restaurant/Team shall have no rights, and *Event Name* shall have no obligations, under the said Participation Agreement. Upon such termination, *Event Name* may retain as liquidated damages all or any portion of the fee previously paid by the participating Restaurant/Team under said Participation Agreement and may, in its sole discretion, permit any other person to use the space reserved by the participating Restaurant/Team.
13. The participating Restaurant/Team agrees to accept as conclusive and binding the decision of *Event Name* as to any dispute between participating Restaurant/Team and any other participating Restaurant/Team or any person attending *Event Name* or as to any matter not covered by these Terms of Participation Agreement.
14. *Event Name* shall not be responsible for any loss due to problems with equipment, supplies or general power failures.

Guidelines for Health Precautions

Permits. Each Restaurant/Team complying with the attached guidelines will be provided with a temporary health permit at no cost for the day of the event. Permits will be issued prior to the event. If the actual set-up on site does not comply with the guidelines, immediate corrections will be required or the permit will be revoked.

Temperature. Foods requiring refrigeration must be maintained at 45°F or colder on a constant basis. Portable coolers are acceptable if constantly drained to remain dry. Refrigeration trucks at a specified location will be available. Hot foods must be maintained at a constant temperature of 130°F or hotter. Covered crockpots are acceptable if food is put into crockpot to maintain temperature. Raw meat must be imbedded in ice (as opposed to sitting on top of ice) and must maintain 45°F or less throughout meat. You must provide a numerically scaled probe-type product thermometer 0–220°F scale (available at restaurant supply dealers.)

Hot and Cold Water, Hand Washing, and Toilets. Event sponsors will provide portable toilets. Sinks for washing pots and pans will be made available. It will be essential for Restaurant/Team management to insure that their staff uses these facilities for all pots or utensils that become soiled and will be reused, and that persons preparing or serving food wash their hands on a regular basis. A container of water with a spigot, soap, and disposable towels will be required in each area for hand washing.

Protection from Insects and Vermin. Protection from insects may take the form of electric fly protectors, screening from prevailing winds, covers over food preparation areas, or others as suggested by Restaurants/Teams. Overall control will require extremely careful control of liquid and solid wastes, and provisions that food not be left in exposed areas.

Waste Receptacles. Sponsors will provide covered solid waste receptacles and a liquid waste disposal system. All waste receptacles used by Restaurants/Teams should be covered at all times and emptied regularly into central disposal facilities.

Coverage of Foods. All food products must be wrapped or stored in protected cases or cupboards except when it is actually being prepared or served. Keep on site food preparation to a minimum (e.g., cutting, chopping). Grills, frying pans, or other cooking devices must be covered when not in use. Overhead protection (e.g., tent) is required. Call *Event Name* if you need help in securing shelter.

Sensitive Foods. Certain types of foods present special health hazards and will require specific discussion with the Health Department on appropriate precautions and safeguards. These include

- Pork, which must be cooked and maintained at high temperatures (over 150°F internal temperature).
- Poultry, which must be maintained at higher temperatures (165°F or more) and must be handled with extreme care to avoid cross-contamination between cooked and uncooked food.

Additional requirements may be necessary. These guidelines intend to allow as great a flexibility as possible for outdoor food preparation and service without creating undue health risks. Exceptions or alternative solutions to any of the problem areas outlined here are encouraged, but will require advanced discussion and approval by the health department.

IT IS THE RESPONSIBILITY OF EACH PARTICIPATING RESTAURANT/TEAM TO CONTACT THE HEALTH DEPARTMENT.

Appendix 10.3: Annual Chili Cook-Off Registration Form

Registration is now being held for the *Event Name* Chili Cook-Off. Teams may enter the Professional Category at a fee of $50 or the Novice Category at a fee of $35.

Early Registration Deadline: *Friday, Date.* (Teams registering after this deadline will be subject to a $25 late registration fee).

Late Registration Deadline: *Friday, Date.* ***No applications will be accepted after this date—No exceptions.***

Chili Cook-Off Will Be Held: *Friday, Date* from 9:00 a.m. until 9:00 p.m. on Main Street in downtown Anytown.

Agreement to Participate

By this agreement duly signed ______________________________ (Name of Establishment or Team Name) officially confirms its participation in the *Event Name* Chili Cook-Off.

It is agreed that all rules and regulations attached to this agreement are a part thereof and that no agreement other than those contained herein shall be binding on the parties unless in writing, signed by an official of *Event Name*. The applicable deposit of $50 Professional/$35 Novice must accompany this agreement and is due no later than *Friday, Date*. If applying after this date, please add a late fee charge of $25.

(Please Print)

Establishment or Team Name: ______________________________

Address: ______________________________

City, State, and Zip Code: ______________________________

Phone: ____________________ Fax: ____________________

Name of Head Cook: ______________________________

Signature of Head Cook: ____________________ Date: __________

Appendix 10.4: Annual Chili Cook-Off Official Judging Sheet

Novice (Score on a Scale of 1–10)

Chili	Team Spirit	Appearance	Taste x 2	Total
#1				
#2				
#3				
#4				
#5				
#6				
#7				
#8				
#9				
#10				
#11				
#12				
#13				
#14				
#15				

Appendix 10.5: Ice Carving Competition Rules and Regulations

1. Check-in for all competitors will be between 10:00 a.m. and 11:00 a.m. on *Day, Month Date* at the corner of Main Street and South Street in downtown Anytown.

2. Judging will take place immediately following conclusion of the competition. All tools and identification must be removed from the carving areas before the judging begins.

3. Each competitor may utilize no more than one helper. The helper may handle the ice and your tools; however, he or she cannot touch or handle the ice with any tools other than ice tongs.

4. There will be a two-hour time limit for professionals for completion of their sculpture. There will be a 1.5-hour time limit for novices to complete their sculpture.

5. Ice blocks and electrical power will be provided. Please notify us at *(800) 555–1234* as soon as possible if you will require power. Tools must be provided by the individual competitors. If electrical chainsaws are to be used, the competitor must supply their own grounded, three-prong extension cord.

6. No artificial props, decorations, lights, or coloring of ice will be allowed. Special carving platforms will be provided.

7. A maximum of 30 positions (15 professional and 15 novice) approximately 10-foot by 10-foot will be assigned on a first-come, first-serve basis. A sign will be provided to list your name and/or organization.

8. ***Remember—Safety First!*** Each participant is responsible for his or her own safety, as well as the safety of other competitors and the general public. For personal safety, we suggest rubber boots and taped extension cords. The competition director reserves the right to remove any sculpture and/or participant determined to be a safety hazard.

9. Height Restriction: For safety reasons, sculptures are to be no more than 10-feet high.

10. Violation of any rules will result in disqualification.

11. The decision of the judges is final.

12. ***Sportsmanship Rule***: Any contestant may be ejected for unsportsmanlike behavior, as deemed by the Ice Carving Competition Director.

Appendix 10.6: Jalapeño Eating Contest Rules and Regulations

1. All contestants must sign a waiver of liability against *Event Name*, Anytown, USA.

2. Each contestant will be provided 20 jalapeño peppers.

3. Size of jalapeño peppers will be random.

4. Contestants are given 60 seconds—The individual who eats the most peppers in 60 seconds (or finishes their 20 peppers first) will be declared the winner.

5. All finished stems must be placed back onto each contestant's plate and will be measured for qualification.

6. Any finished stem with more than 1 millimeter of remaining pepper will not count toward the overall total.

Appendix 10.7: Food Festival Restaurant Pentathlon Rules and Procedures

Each restaurant receives points for placing first through tenth in the following events:

- Waiter's Race
- Silver Spoon
- Tent Decorating
- Bartender's Mix-Off
- Chef Cook-Off

Scoring is as follows:

First place	11 points	Sixth place	5 points
Second place	9 points	Seventh place	4 points
Third place	8 points	Eighth place	3 points
Fourth place	7 points	Ninth place	2 points
Fifth place	6 points	Tenth place	1 point

If a restaurant places more than one individual in first through tenth place in the Waiter's Race or Bartender's Contest, only the highest score will apply towards the pentathlon total.

Example

Waiter's Race (Finish Results) Pentathlon Points

Restaurant # 1	Restaurant # 1—11 points
Restaurant # 2	Restaurant # 2— 9 points
Restaurant # 3	Restaurant # 3— 8 points

Each restaurant will have the opportunity to drop their lowest score.

The top scores in each category will be added together for the pentathlon total.

The restaurant with the most points wins first place. Prize money is as follows:

1st Place: $500 and Trophy
2nd Place: $300
3rd Place: $200

Appendix 10.8: People's Choice Award Ballot

Thank you for taking part in the People's Choice Award. Your response will help to determine who has the best food to offer at this year's food festival. Listed below alphabetically are the restaurants present at this year's festival. Please place an X on the line beside the ONE restaurant that you feel offers the BEST TASTING FOOD at this year's festival. We appreciate your participation.

_______ Name of Restaurant

_______ Name of Restaurant

_______ Name of Restaurant

_______ Name of Restaurant

_______ Name of Restaurant

_______ Name of Restaurant

_______ Name of Restaurant

_______ Name of Restaurant

_______ Name of Restaurant

_______ Name of Restaurant

_______ Name of Restaurant

_______ Name of Restaurant

_______ Name of Restaurant

_______ Name of Restaurant

_______ Name of Restaurant

_______ Name of Restaurant

_______ Name of Restaurant

_______ Name of Restaurant

Chapter 11
Event Ideas—Holiday Celebrations

Put a new spin on holiday festivities by creating a new event or adding elements to an existing one. Holiday events help bring communities and families together to observe traditional celebrations. Combine numerous activities together to create an exciting, new holiday happening in your community.

Luck o' the Irish

Irish Jig Contest—This is a great addition to the community St. Patrick's Day Celebration. A green hat is given to all participants, and a member of the local Irish Club serves as a judge. Irish music is played while all participants dance—no partners needed. When the judge taps a contestant on the shoulder, they are out. The last one dancing wins a prize.

St. Patrick's Day Celebration and Parade—Everyone wears their green and comes to find the luck o' the Irish by bringing their Irish spirit. Start the day's activities with a traditional parade, which features marching bands, bagpipe music, step dancers, tall shamrocks, Irish breeds of dogs, horses, and floats. An exciting spin on the parade is to host a "baby buggy" or "red wagon parade" and to keep motorized vehicles to a minimum. Families decorate their buggies or wagons and dress in costume as they march in the parade. If possible, get the local traffic department to paint the center line of the parade route emerald green for the marchers to follow. Before or after the parade, organizers may sponsor a *Little Miss and Little Mr. Leprechaun Contest* with the most authentic looking boy and girl leprechaun in each age category (0–2 years old, 3–4 years old, 5–7 years old) winning a $100 saving bond. Participants enjoy the smells of corned beef and cabbage when offered Irish food and drink specials along with nontraditional Irish games such as a hairy-leg contest, keg toss, and bowling down Guinness cans with a cabbage. Children enjoy painting a mural featuring shamrocks, leprechauns, and a pot of gold. Drawings for prizes or raffles can feature products imported from Ireland or, better yet, a trip to Ireland.

Search for the Lost Leprechaun—Participants go on a treasure hunt while taking a hike through the woods looking for the lost leprechaun and pot of gold.

Wearing o' the Green—Host a contest at the St. Patrick's Day events for the best green outfit, best Irish outfit, or best leprechaun outfit, in both adult and children's divisions.

Here Comes Peter Cottontail

Breakfast With Peter Cottontail—Participants may join Peter for a continental breakfast and storytelling. After breakfast, each child makes an Easter craft and has his or her picture taken with Peter Cottontail.

Dinosaur Day—This event is an innovative way to compete with other Easter activities. The event planner hosts a dinosaur egg hunt using plastic eggs filled with candy. One egg should be marked in each age group as the "dinosaur egg." The child who finds the dinosaur egg receives a giant egg filled with candy. Related activities: Throw a *Dinosaur Party* with dinosaur cookies, dinosaur mask making, and dinosaur puppets. A mock archeological dig for dinosaur "bones" may be added by using a wooden dinosaur skeleton puzzle. Important materials to remember include masks, puppets, construction paper, glue, markers, and crayons.

Easter Egg Plunge—This event is designed for communities with warm spring weather or a heated indoor pool. A hot glue gun is used to glue a nut to the bottom of one half of a plastic egg to provide weight to sink the egg. Drill two holes in the other half of the egg, then the two halves are hot glued together to keep them from coming apart. One hundred plastic eggs are submerged in the pool. At the sound of the whistle, a group is given two minutes to retrieve as many eggs as they can from the water.

Easter Marshmallow Drop—30,000 marshmallows are dropped out of a helicopter onto a field. Six special eggs are dropped with them and turned in for a special prize.

Egg Scramble—This is a fun name for the traditional Easter egg hunt. The day is filled with an egg toss, egg on the spoon, and egg eating, making the activities *eggciting* for all. Participants enjoy prizes, goodies, a bonnet/hat contest, and a magic show. The Easter Bunny also makes an appearance.

Eggstravaganza—It's all about eggs! Participants learn egg decorating, marbling, and batiking. Activities include egg tossing, egg on spoon, making bunny ears, bunny hop race, and the famous egg hunt. Serve egg salad for refreshment.

Hunt 'n Lunch With the Easter Bunny—This event may become an annual Easter egg hunt and lunch for children age 3 to 10. Hotdogs, chips, and a drink are served after the children find all of the hidden eggs.

Late Night Easter Egg Search—This is a perfect event to involve preteens in the Easter Holiday. Participants use flashlights to find eggs (filled with coupons for prizes and gifts) hidden throughout the park.

Summertime Fun

Highlight a variety of family-oriented activities for the community to enjoy. Activities include bicycle rodeo, create a flag, face painting, mural painting, stupid pet tricks, watermelon seed spitting contest, mask making, photo exhibition and competition, neighborhood theme song competition, and pet and owner look-a-like contests. Physical activities include tug-of-war, big wheel race, an obstacle course, tee ball, beanbag throw, and sack races. Everyone gets a goodie bag with small toy, prizes, or candy. The day's festivities culminate with a spectacular fireworks display.

Bike Rodeo—These timed bike games include slalom, parallel, slow race, obstacle drop, and relay races.

Block of Ice Contest—The luckiest person who guesses the time it will take for a huge block of ice to melt wins a prize. The local ice company may sponsor by donating a 1,500-pound block of ice to your summer event.

Diaper Derby—Parents encourage their babies, 6 to 12 months of age, to crawl across the finish line by waving a favorite rattle or teddy bear. A variety of prizes can be awarded to the winners.

Fourth of July Pied Piper Parade—Invite children to bring their horns, whistles, and other music instruments to open the Fourth of July celebration.

Fourth of July Parade—The parade includes minifloats carrying costumed children, marching units, decorated bicycles, tricycles, and wheelchairs. A minifloat often begins with a red wagon as the wheels are already there. Categories to be judged include best wagon float, costume, bike, trike, stroller, wheelchair, or band.

Great Texas Steak Out—Everything planned is REALLY BIG! Using a western theme, a big dinner is included, with lots of food, contests, games, and entertainment. Big food could include half-pound hamburgers or 20-ounce steak, jumbo baked potatoes, huge dill pickles, and giant glasses of iced tea. The contests includes a chili cook-off, best rib competition, best sauce competition, hog calling, log rolling, silver dollar pitching, 10-gallon hat contest, watermelon seed spitting contest, woodcarving contest, lasso instruction, and competition. Plan games such as ring toss (using hula hoops for rings), goofy golf (using jumbo clubs), 55-gallon drum bucking bronco ride (25-gallon for children), and country dancing.

Ice Cream Crank Off—Groups register as a team and compete in various categories, including fastest finish, best ice cream, and most unusual flavor. Each team brings their own supplies but must prepare the ice cream mix in front of the judges. After the judging is final, ice cream cones are sold or given away.

Incredible Water Fight—Participants have a blast with water guns, balloons, and water activities.

Kids' Kick Off—Young children enjoy a chance to show off their skills at kicking a ball to the finish line. Planners should provide prizes for all participants.

Mini-Indy—And they're off! Big wheels, tricycles or similar riding toys (without motors) are the race cars for this Mini-Indy 500. Participants, ages 3 to 5, must furnish their own vehicles.

Mini-Marathon—Two teams of any age compete in 10 to 20 events (e.g., watermelon eating, frisbee toss, basketball throw, raisin count). Each participant is stationed at an event. When one participant finishes an event, he or she runs to the next station and begins that event until all events are completed.

My Country: Red, White, and Blue—Using patriotic-colored materials, children create what freedom means to them.

Sports Spectacular—This event features sports of every kind (including crazy events for the less athletically inclined). Ideas include the old time favorites like three-legged races, cartwheel competitions, sack races, and spoon races, croquet, bocce, and horseshoes.

Super Splits—What better way to beat the heat than a giant banana split? Four to five banquet tables are set up with 10-foot plastic rain gutters placed in line so that there is one long gutter on each side of the table. The gutters are lined with aluminum foil and filled with ice cream. Participants select their own toppings from the variety of condiments brought in by members of your neighborhood (e.g., whipped cream, nuts, cherries, syrups). Gutters are easy to wash out and may be saved for years. An added activity could be to make homemade ice-cream earlier in the day.

Thin Air Festival—Contests or free plays are made available for the following activities: remote control airplanes, darts, kite flying, boomerangs, frisbees, paper airplanes, yo-yos, Hacky Sacks, and balloon volleyball. A particularly fun activity for children is a *Balloon Sculpture* in which children (and adults) add long blown-up balloons to a structure that has been started prior to the opening of the festival. Balloons can be added by tying onto an existing balloon or by stuffing a balloon in between other balloons.

Treasure Hunt—"Yo ho ho" and treasure chest full of coins. This belongs to the first person who locates the buried treasure. Each team receives a treasure map and gathers clues along the way. The final clue requires calculation as to the exact spot to dig to reduce the likelihood of multiple holes being dug in the neighborhood.

Wacky Olympics—Include events such as rubber chicken throw, shoe kick, marshmallow shot put, straw javelin, paper plate discus, blindfolded putting contest, playing softball with a Ping-Pong paddle, beachball volleyball (play under a water sprinkler on a hot day), and armless events (tie arms behind backs).

Goblins, Ghosts, and Witches

Children's Pumpkin Decorating—Each child can purchase a pumpkin or bring their own to paint for Halloween. Provide supplies such as markers, glue, pipe cleaners, yarn, felt, glue, sponges, and toothpicks.

Great Pumpkin Patch—This is a ghoulishly good time with scary costumes, a hay maze, live entertainment, and a ***Pumpkin Carving Contest*** (awards for most traditional jack o' lantern, most innovative abstract design, and most recognizable national or local celebrity). Offer pumpkins for sale, and include a scarecrow making workshop, hayrides, a pie-eating contest, a giant pumpkin weigh-in, and all the pumpkin pies the community can eat.

Halloween Boo in the Zoo—This is an alternative to traditional trick-or-treating. Participants come to the zoo for an evening of trick-or-treating at each animal "house," fun games, face painting, walking through the Happy Halloween House, magic show, the ***Halloween Costume Contest,*** and ***Halloween Parade*** (prizes may be awarded for scariest costume, best animated character, most colorful costume, most original costume, or most authentic costume).

Halloween Howl/Fright Night/Scared Silly—Have participants come dressed in Halloween costumes and enjoy the fun. A scavenger hunt, spooky games, and Halloween treats await you in the Pumpkin Patch.

Halloween Fun Fest—Participants wear their Halloween costumes and join in for a fun safe event for preschoolers. The event planner should include snacks, a costume parade and contest, and Halloween activities.

Halloween Parade/Halloween Hoot—Calling all goblins to dress in their favorite costume and march down Main Street. A ghoulish evening is spent downtown with the festivities beginning with ghost stories and continued with a parade of all costumed creatures. Children receive complimentary bags to go trick or treating in downtown stores after the parade. In addition to the parade, a ***Halloween Window Painting Contest*** is offered, where merchants paint their storefront windows and compete in a ***Pumpkin Carving Contest***. Local celebrities, the mayor, and city council members serve as judges and give awards. Additional elements can include a ***Halloween Costume Contest***, pumpkin carving classes, and a ***Backyard Carnival*** for kids.

Haunted Campfire—Friendly monsters howl and growl for a monstrously good time. Start the evening with a bone-chilling tale while participants sit around the campfire. Creatively carved pumpkins are used to decorate around the fire. Offer treats to everyone.

Haunted Trails and Scary Tales/Hobgoblin Hike (Scare Trail, Haunted Forest)—Decorate the community park with spooktacular attractions and activities. Participants can walk or take a hayride through the park while listening to spooky tales. Create different "scare stations" throughout the park. Planners may include a mattress buried just underground and covered with hay to create a very effective jolt on a walking trail. Organizers may also include a graveyard, with tombstones created out of cardboard and fluorescent paint. Sounds of wind, rustling leaves, rocks in tin cans, and groaning ghouls help create a gloomy environment. An open casket donated by local funeral home with a volunteer playing the role of a corpse inside, witches brewing with a cast iron pot, and a werewolf, who hides behind the trees with sound effects to make the hair stand on the back of participants necks will all add to the event.

Guests get caught by spider webs created with fishing line hung from tree branches. Another station can portray a tomb for participants to enter built out of black polyethylene plastic suspended from trees. Attach a strobe light to disorient the guests.

Build a ***Mysterious Maze*** out of cardboard and plywood walls, with knee-high holes in the cardboard, ghouls grab at the participants with hands. Use a strobe light deep in the trees (100 yards) just so guests wonder about what it is. Chemical glow sticks may be used by placing them in unusual spaces and made objects (such as irregular balls of tissue paper). Standard "scenes" may be spotlighted for effect; however, darkness is very effective. Noise from chainsaws (remove the chain), blowers, and firecrackers can startle even the brave. Dimly lit scenes with figures moving slowly about or construct figures pulled on wires. The darkness hides the wires and operators and makes it more real.

Construct bats and snakes (with red or green diode eyes) with hooks for easy hanging and battery pack for lights and movement. Simple designs are installed in bunches with placement back into trees. All "creatures" do not have to be recognizable, and the unknown is certainly more mysterious than the known.

The evenings are planned for teens, but the day is saved for younger children. Enchanted cottage or forest at the end of the path for ages six and under is a great addition. Planners may also include storybook characters, a story glen with Mother Goose, treats from elves behind trees, a wishing well, a puppet show in the trees, and wrapped candy hanging from a gold tree.

Haunted House Hunt—The event organizer coproduces with a local radio station that will give out clues to the specific location of the haunted house. Different rooms are decorated to feature examples of ghoulish, ghostly, and haunted themes. Design a maze in one room where guests feel their way through the room while experiencing unexpected noises, creatures, twists, and turns.

Hollywood Scares—This makes for a fun spin off of "Hollywood Squares" for a Halloween event. A set made out of cardboard and scaffolding is made to look like an old castle with nine windows cut out. Participants and the game host dress up in Halloween costumes. Use questions dealing with Halloween trivia.

Jack o' Squirt Contest—Participants try to extinguish the flame inside a carved pumpkin using a squirt gun. The person with the best time wins the pumpkin or Halloween prize pack.

Lunch With the Great Pumpkin—Calling all ghosts and goblins! Children come in costumes for trick-or-treating, carnival games, a magic show, a not-very-scary house, and plenty of tricks and treats.

Monster Mash/Lil' Boo Bash/Halloween Boozaar—A Halloween party featuring Halloween games such as pin the wart on the witch (like pin the tail on the donkey; the wart is a gumball or piece of bubble gum), drop the clothes pin in a pumpkin, cake walk on paper stones with witches and ghost painted on them, face-painting for those without masks, crafts, prizes, and refreshments. The highlight of the event is the Monster Mash costume dance featuring scary music. For those who do not engage in dancing, Halloween movie classics such as *It's the Great Pumpkin, Charlie Brown* or *Casper Saves Halloween* may be offered.

Pumpkinfest/Pumpkin Patch—Celebrate the harvest season with events relating to pumpkins, such as a pumpkin carving contest, children's costume parade, and pumpkin bowling. A wall of pumpkins is made, where participants carve pumpkins and make a wall from the pumpkins, which are all lit at the same time. Festival-goers win prizes for guessing the weight of a pumpkin, playing cow-patty bingo, and winning the wheelbarrow race (winding paths are lined with pumpkins and the blindfolded driver has to negotiate the course by following directions of the rider). Everyone enjoys pumpkin pies, pumpkin ice cream and other edible pumpkin delights. A *Pumpkin Painting Contest,* in which participants purchase a pumpkin on-site and then decorate the pumpkin with supplies provided, may also be added. Award prizes to the artist for funniest, scariest, most creative, most original, and best of show. All participants get to take their decorated pumpkin home or can donate to a children's home or other charity.

Scarecrow Row—Assign employees or merchants in a downtown area a lightpole to compete in the "decorate a lightpole like a scarecrow" contest to be held prior to the evenings festivities. Entrants win prizes and ribbons for creativity, best display, and so forth. Examples include best live scarecrow, family of scarecrows, and scarecrows climbing the light pole.

Things That Go Bump in the Night—Storytellers tell stories and legends of ghosts. The evening can be highlighted with a candlelight tour of the local cemetery or historic building.

Trunk or Treat—Cars line up at a location (e.g., church, recreation center) for kids to trick or treat around the trunks of the cars. An entertaining alternative is to feature classic cars with all drivers dressed in Halloween or period costumes.

Gobble, Gobble, Gobble

Fowl Shot Contest—Hold a free-throw shooting contest around the Thanksgiving holiday. Winners of each division get a certificate for a free turkey from a local grocer. Divide participants into grade divisions for competition: K–1, 2–3, 4–5, 6–8, 9–12 and adults. Participants give a $1 donation for as many sets of shots as time allows. All collected money goes to local food bank for Thanksgiving dinner.

Turkey Calling Contest—Participants come dressed in their best hunting wear and compete in both professional and amateur categories. Each caller is required to know five calls for the competition. Determine the order of callers by the draw, and the top 10 in each category enter the finals. Decorate the stage as an outdoor setting and select professionals involved in conservation, hunting, and outdoor activities to judge. Planners should invite outdoor, hunting gear, and equipment vendors to be exhibitors during the contest.

Turkey Hunt—Participants (ages 12 and up) do not need camo and ammunition to hunt these turkeys. He or she just listens and looks for clues to win a turkey from the grocery store for Thanksgiving.

Turkey Fry Contest—Invite chefs to bring out their cherished fried turkey recipe and turkey fryer for the newest contest in town. For $2 guests can sample the turkey and vote for the prize-winning favorite.

Turkey Waddle—In this Thanksgiving relay race participants dress with inner tubes over their clothes and swimming fins on their feet. A goofy hat adds to the silly costume.

Sights and Sounds of Christmas

Christmas Lights Tour/Grand Illumination Tour—The event planner organizes a bus tour for seniors who may not be able to drive around at night on their own. Tour all the local Christmas light favorites while serving hot chocolate, eggnog, and Christmas cookies.

Christmas in the City: A Downtown Tradition—Form a downtown holiday committee to bring more visitors to the downtown during the holidays and to make Christmas extra special for the community. Transform downtown into a winter wonderland rich with tradition and full of activity. Planners may include an outdoor ice-skating rink, numerous special events, themes, window decorating, and holiday activities. Create a brochure and poster listing the events and activities to be held during the entire month of December. Distribute the promotional materials to local businesses and residents, as well as the visitor's center.

The downtown comes alive with holiday spirit, as the annual *Light Up the City* event takes place. Spectators are dazzled with a display of holiday lights down Main Street and with a fireworks show to end the evening with a bang. Horse-drawn carriages are always a popular hit for any community, while the smell of hot cocoa and apple cider is in the air and the sounds of laughter of children fill the streets. The storefronts are decorated for the season with the artwork from local schoolchildren who participate in ***Windows of Opportunity***, a children's painting gallery program. A special treat is added for visitors with live mannequins as window displays. Students from the local theater or community ballet wear costumes from their current shows or the stores' holiday outfits.

The holiday events and activities held during the month of December included the following:

- *Caroling in the Commons*
- *Cocoa and Holiday Treats*
- *Cookie Decorating Contest*
- *Downtown Giving Tree*
- *Horse-drawn Carriage Rides With Santa*
- *Jingle Bell Walk/Run*
- *Restaurant Holiday Baking Contest*
- *Storefront Decorating Contest*
- *Yule Log Lighting and Bonfire*

Christmas in the Park/Holiday Trail of Lights/ Garden of Light—The local park or botanical garden is decorated with lights, featuring hundreds of thousands of lights on park trees and a luminary path leading participants to a fantasy land of carolers, musicians, marshmallow roasting, storytelling, puppet shows, and of course good ole St. Nick.

Festival of Lights—This is a holiday tradition to bring families and visitors to downtown. Instead of a tree lighting ceremony, one may try lighting a forest of trees for a brighter and more magnificent exhibition. A parade (*City Lights, Holiday Nights*) with decorated floats, bands, and costumed characters all lit for the occasion, is included.

Festival of Trees—Invite florists, interior designers, and other groups from the community to decorate trees sponsored by local businesses and civic organizations. Designate a theme, such as "Sights and Sounds of Christmas."

Holiday Festival of Lights—Feature a driving tour through a popular community park containing light displays, with events and attractions such as marshmallow roasting over an open fire, enchanted forest walking trail, train rides, and photos with Santa. Plan a nighttime road race with participants receiving glow-in-the-dark necklaces, shoestrings, or other souvenirs. The course can be lined with luminarics and numcrous light displays to add an extra effect.

Light Up the City/Tree Lighting Ceremony—A wonderful way to start the holiday festivities right before a nighttime Christmas Parade. Invite a local choir to lead the audience in singing Christmas carols. The Mayor and other local dignitaries gather to light the city tree. A wonderful addition is to entice downtown shop owners to decorate their storefronts with lights and simultaneously turn their lights on when the officials light the tree. Local merchants serve hot cider and Christmas cookies to all.

Santa's Village—Children meet with Santa and his elves to discuss their Christmas wishes while parents take pictures and videos. Other activities include ***Christmas Card House***, where children make their own Christmas cards, face painting, caricature artists, and the ***Toy Room***, displaying an assortment of nutcrackers, old fashioned wooden toys, trains, stuffed animals, and handmade dolls.

References and Resources

Allen, L. R., Kraus, R. G., and Williams, A. D. (1986). *Philadelphia recreation volunteerism project final report: A research and demonstration project.* Philadelphia, PA: Temple University, Department of Recreation and Leisure Studies.

Berlonghi, A. (1990). *The special event risk management manual*. Self-published. Dana Point, CA: Author.

Catherwood, D. W. and Van Kirk, R. L. (1992). *The complete guide to special event management*. New York, NY: John Wiley & Sons.

Delemere, T. and Hinch, T. (1994). Community festivals: Celebration or sellout? *Recreation Canada, 52*(1), 26–29.

Foster, J. S. (1998). *Book two: The law of meetings, conventions and trade shows.* Atlanta, GA: Author.

Getz, D. (1991). *Festivals, special events, and tourism.* New York, NY: Van Nostrand Reinhold.

Getz, D. (1997). *Event management & event tourism.* New York, NY: Cognizant Communications Corporation.

Getz, D. and Frisby, W. (1988). Evaluating management effectiveness in community run festivals. *Journal of Travel Research, 27*(1), 22–27.

Hinch, T. and Delemere, T. (1993). Native festivals as tourism attractions: A community challenge. *Journal of Applied Recreation Research, 18*(2), 131–142.

Jackson, R. and Schmader, S. W. (1991). *Special events: Inside and out—A "how-to" approach to event production, marketing and sponsorship.* Champaign, IL: Sagamore Publishing.

Mayfield, T. L. and Crompton, J. L. (1995). Development of an instrument for identifying community reasons for staging a festival. *Journal of Travel Research, 34*(1), 37–44.

McCurley, S. (1995). *Working effectively with volunteers.* Unpublished Manuscript.

Paumier, C. (1988). *Designing the successful downtown.* Washington, DC: The Urban Land Institute.

Robinson, A. and Noel, J. G. (1991). Research needs for festivals: A management perspective. *Journal of Applied Recreation Research, 16*(1), 78–88.

About the Authors

Angie Prosser has spent her professional career planning and facilitating events in Greenville, South Carolina. She is the Program and Events Administrator for the City of Greenville and serves on numerous event boards of directors and planning committees. Angie has a bachelor of science degree and a master's degree in Parks, Recreation, and Tourism Management from Clemson University. She has more than 16 years experience in special event planning, facilitating over 100 events a year.

Angie is an NRPA-certified Parks and Recreation Professional and currently serves as President of the South Carolina Festival and Event Association. She also served as President of South Carolina Recreation and Parks Association (SCRPA) and was selected as SCRPA Young Professional of the Year in 1990 and SCRPA Professional of the Year in 1995. She is co-author of *Great Special Events and Activities*, published by Venture Publishing. Angie is a regular speaker at special event, recreation, and nonprofit conferences covering all topics relating to event planning. Angie can often be found fly-fishing, gardening, hiking, and spending quality time with her close friends.

Ashli Rutledge is currently a Media Buyer/Planner at The Leslie Agency in Greenville, South Carolina, one of the oldest and largest advertising firms in the Southeast. Ashli holds a bachelor of science degree in Parks, Recreation, and Tourism Management with an emphasis in travel and tourism from Clemson University. She began her "event" career at Freedom Weekend Aloft in Greenville, South Carolina. In addition, Ashli has worked as Sales and Marketing Director at Greenville Events, Inc. and Promotions Director at WESC-FM. When not working, Ashli enjoys reading, music, outdoor activities, and spending time with her son, Ivan.

Books by Venture Publishing, Inc.

The A•B•Cs of Behavior Change: Skills for Working with Behavior Problems in Nursing Homes
by Margaret D. Cohn, Michael A. Smyer, and Ann L. Horgas

Activity Experiences and Programming within Long-Term Care
by Ted Tedrick and Elaine R. Green

The Activity Gourmet
by Peggy Powers

Advanced Concepts for Geriatric Nursing Assistants
by Carolyn A. McDonald

Adventure Programming
edited by John C. Miles and Simon Priest

Assessment: The Cornerstone of Activity Programs
by Ruth Perschbacher

Behavior Modification in Therapeutic Recreation: An Introductory Manual
by John Datillo and William D. Murphy

Benefits of Leisure
edited by B. L. Driver, Perry J. Brown, and George L. Peterson

Benefits of Recreation Research Update
by Judy M. Sefton and W. Kerry Mummery

Beyond Bingo: Innovative Programs for the New Senior
by Sal Arrigo, Jr., Ann Lewis, and Hank Mattimore

Beyond Bingo 2: More Innovative Programs for the New Senior
by Sal Arrigo, Jr.

Both Gains and Gaps: Feminist Perspectives on Women's Leisure
by Karla Henderson, M. Deborah Bialeschki, Susan M. Shaw, and Valeria J. Freysinger

Client Assessment in Therapeutic Recreation Services
by Norma J. Stumbo

Conceptual Foundations for Therapeutic Recreation
edited by David R. Austin, John Dattilo, and Bryan P. McCormick

Dementia Care Programming: An Identity-Focused Approach
by Rosemary Dunne

Dimensions of Choice: A Qualitative Approach to Recreation, Parks, and Leisure Research
by Karla A. Henderson

Diversity and the Recreation Profession: Organizational Perspectives
edited by Maria T. Allison and Ingrid E. Schneider

Effective Management in Therapeutic Recreation Service
by Gerald S. O'Morrow and Marcia Jean Carter

Evaluating Leisure Services: Making Enlightened Decisions, Second Edition
by Karla A. Henderson and M. Deborah Bialeschki

Everything From A to Y: The Zest Is up to You! Older Adult Activities for Every Day of the Year
by Nancy R. Cheshire and Martha L. Kenney

The Evolution of Leisure: Historical and Philosophical Perspectives
by Thomas Goodale and Geoffrey Godbey

Experience Marketing: Strategies for the New Millennium
by Ellen L. O'Sullivan and Kathy J. Spangler

Facilitation Techniques in Therapeutic Recreation
by John Dattilo

File o' Fun: A Recreation Planner for Games & Activities, Third Edition
by Jane Harris Ericson and Diane Ruth Albright

The Game and Play Leader's Handbook: Facilitating Fun and Positive Interaction
by Bill Michaelis and John M. O'Connell

The Game Finder—A Leader's Guide to Great Activities
by Annette C. Moore

Getting People Involved in Life and Activities: Effective Motivating Techniques
by Jeanne Adams

Glossary of Recreation Therapy and Occupational Therapy
by David R. Austin

Great Special Events and Activities
by Annie Morton, Angie Prosser, and Sue Spangler

Group Games & Activity Leadership
by Kenneth J. Bulik

Growing With Care: Using Greenery, Gardens, and Nature with Aging and Special Populations
by Betsy Kreidler

Hands on! Children's Activities for Fairs, Festivals, and Special Events
by Karen L. Ramey

Inclusive Leisure Services: Responding to the Rights of People with Disabilities, Second Edition
by John Dattilo

Innovations: A Recreation Therapy Approach to Restorative Programs
by Dawn R. De Vries and Julie M. Lake

Internships in Recreation and Leisure Services: A Practical Guide for Students, Third Edition
by Edward E. Seagle, Jr. and Ralph W. Smith

Interpretation of Cultural and Natural Resources, Second Edition
by Douglas M. Knudson, Ted T. Cable, and Larry Beck

Intervention Activities for At-Risk Youth
by Norma J. Stumbo

Introduction to Recreation and Leisure Services, Eighth Edition
by Karla A. Henderson, M. Deborah Bialeschki, John L. Hemingway, Jan S. Hodges, Beth D. Kivel, and H. Douglas Sessoms

Introduction to Writing Goals and Objectives: A Manual for Recreation Therapy Students and Entry-Level Professionals
by Suzanne Melcher

Leadership and Administration of Outdoor Pursuits, Second Edition
by Phyllis Ford and James Blanchard

Leadership in Leisure Services: Making a Difference, Second Edition
by Debra J. Jordan

Leisure and Leisure Services in the 21st Century
by Geoffrey Godbey

The Leisure Diagnostic Battery: Users Manual and Sample Forms
by Peter A. Witt and Gary Ellis

Leisure Education I: A Manual of Activities and Resources, Second Edition
by Norma J. Stumbo

Leisure Education II: More Activities and Resources, Second Edition
by Norma J. Stumbo

Leisure Education III: More Goal-Oriented Activities
by Norma J. Stumbo

Leisure Education IV: Activities for Individuals with Substance Addictions
by Norma J. Stumbo

Leisure Education Program Planning: A Systematic Approach, Second Edition
by John Dattilo

Leisure Education Specific Programs
by John Dattilo

Leisure in Your Life: An Exploration, Fifth Edition
by Geoffrey Godbey

Leisure Services in Canada: An Introduction, Second Edition
by Mark S. Searle and Russell E. Brayley

Leisure Studies: Prospects for the Twenty-First Century
edited by Edgar L. Jackson and Thomas L. Burton

The Lifestory Re-Play Circle: A Manual of Activities and Techniques
by Rosilyn Wilder

Models of Change in Municipal Parks and Recreation: A Book of Innovative Case Studies
edited by Mark E. Havitz

More Than a Game: A New Focus on Senior Activity Services
by Brenda Corbett

Nature and the Human Spirit: Toward an Expanded Land Management Ethic
edited by B. L. Driver, Daniel Dustin, Tony Baltic, Gary Elsner, and George Peterson

The Organizational Basis of Leisure Participation: A Motivational Exploration
by Robert A. Stebbins

Outdoor Recreation Management: Theory and Application, Third Edition
by Alan Jubenville and Ben Twight

Planning Parks for People, Second Edition
by John Hultsman, Richard L. Cottrell, and Wendy Z. Hultsman

The Process of Recreation Programming Theory and Technique, Third Edition
by Patricia Farrell and Herberta M. Lundegren

Programming for Parks, Recreation, and Leisure Services: A Servant Leadership Approach
by Donald G. DeGraaf, Debra J. Jordan, and Kathy H. DeGraaf

Protocols for Recreation Therapy Programs
edited by Jill Kelland, along with the Recreation Therapy Staff at Alberta Hospital Edmonton

Quality Management: Applications for Therapeutic Recreation
edited by Bob Riley

A Recovery Workbook: The Road Back from Substance Abuse
by April K. Neal and Michael J. Taleff

Recreation and Leisure: Issues in an Era of Change, Third Edition
edited by Thomas Goodale and Peter A. Witt

Recreation Economic Decisions: Comparing Benefits and Costs, Second Edition
by John B. Loomis and Richard G. Walsh

Recreation for Older Adults: Individual and Group Activities
by Judith A. Elliott and Jerold E. Elliott

Recreation Programming and Activities for Older Adults
by Jerold E. Elliott and Judith A. Sorg-Elliott

Reference Manual for Writing Rehabilitation Therapy Treatment Plans
by Penny Hogberg and Mary Johnson

Research in Therapeutic Recreation: Concepts and Methods
edited by Marjorie J. Malkin and Christine Z. Howe

Simple Expressions: Creative and Therapeutic Arts for the Elderly in Long-Term Care Facilities
by Vicki Parsons

A Social History of Leisure Since 1600
by Gary Cross

A Social Psychology of Leisure
by Roger C. Mannell and Douglas A. Kleiber

Steps to Successful Programming: A Student Handbook to Accompany Programming for Parks, Recreation, and Leisure Services
by Donald G. DeGraaf, Debra J. Jordan, and Kathy H. DeGraaf

Stretch Your Mind and Body: Tai Chi as an Adaptive Activity
by Duane A. Crider and William R. Klinger

Therapeutic Activity Intervention with the Elderly: Foundations and Practices
by Barbara A. Hawkins, Marti E. May, and Nancy Brattain Rogers

Therapeutic Recreation and the Nature of Disabilities
by Kenneth E. Mobily and Richard D. MacNeil

Therapeutic Recreation: Cases and Exercises, Second Edition
by Barbara C. Wilhite and M. Jean Keller

Therapeutic Recreation in Health Promotion and Rehabilitation
by John Shank and Catherine Coyle

Therapeutic Recreation in the Nursing Home
by Linda Buettner and Shelley L. Martin

Therapeutic Recreation Protocol for Treatment of Substance Addictions
by Rozanne W. Faulkner

Tourism and Society: A Guide to Problems and Issues
by Robert W. Wyllie

A Training Manual for Americans with Disabilities Act Compliance in Parks and Recreation Settings
by Carol Stensrud

Venture Publishing, Inc.
1999 Cato Avenue
State College, PA 16801
Phone: (814) 234–4561
Fax: (814) 234–1651